Separate but Loyal:
Ethnicity and
Nationalism in China

About the East-West Center

The East-West Center promotes better relations and understanding among the people and nations of the United States, Asia, and the Pacific through cooperative study, research, and dialogue. Established by the U.S. Congress in 1960, the Center serves as a resource for information and analysis on critical issues of common concern, bringing people together to exchange views, build expertise, and develop policy options.

The Center's 21-acre Honolulu campus, adjacent to the University of Hawai'i at Mānoa, is located midway between Asia and the U.S. mainland and features research, residential, and international conference facilities. The Center's Washington, D.C., office focuses on preparing the United States for an era of growing Asia Pacific prominence.

The Center is an independent, public, nonprofit organization with funding from the U.S. government, and additional support provided by private agencies, individuals, foundations, corporations, and governments in the region.

Policy Studies 56

Separate but Loyal:
Ethnicity and Nationalism in China

Wenfang Tang and Gaochao He

Separate but Loyal:
Ethnicity and Nationalism in China
by Wenfang Tang and Gaochao He

ISSN 1547-1349 (print) and 1547-1330 (electronic)
ISBN 978-1-932728-86-6 (print) and 978-1-932728-87-3 (electronic)

East-West Center
1601 East-West Road
Honolulu, Hawai'i 96848-1601
Tel: 808.944.7111
EWCInfo@EastWestCenter.org
EastWestCenter.org/policystudies

The views expressed are those of the author(s) and not necessarily those of the Center.

Hard copies of publications in the series are available through Amazon.com.

In Asia, hard copies of all titles, and electronic copies of Southeast Asia titles, co-published in Singapore, are available through:

Institute of Southeast Asian Studies
30 Heng Mui Keng Terrace
Pasir Panjang Road, Singapore 119614
Email: publish@iseas.edu.sg
Website: http://bookshop.iseas.edu.sg

Contents

Executive Summary

This study compares ethnic identity and nationalism among China's ethnic groups. Following an examination of the ethnic policies under the Qing empire, the Republic of China, and the People's Republic of China, we set out to test two opposing hypotheses on national identity in contemporary China. One hypothesis is centered around the Han-dominant Confucian tradition, while the other is based on the concept of the modern multiethnic Chinese state that originated during the Qing empire.

To test the above hypotheses, we take a multifaceted empirical approach by exploring the extent to which ethnic minorities are sinicized and the meaning of being Chinese. Specifically, we show how strongly different ethnic groups identify with their own languages and how important they perceive learning those languages to be as a way to carry out their respective cultural traditions. Next, we compare how different groups identify with their religions and how much importance they place on continuing their cultural heritage through religious practices. Third, we examine how intragroup identity and intergroup identity are reflected through interethnic marriage among different ethnic groups. Finally, we compare group identity and national identity in China with those in the United States and Russia, two countries with similarly dominant ethnic majorities and sizable ethnic minorities.

One barrier to the study of ethnic relations in China is the difficulty of collecting systematic and comparable data among the ethnic groups. This study is based on a 2006–2007 questionnaire survey of nearly 1,600 students in 17 high schools. It covers some of the most politically sensitive ethnic groups in China, including the Uyghurs, the Tibetans, the Mongols, the Huis, and the Kazaks, as well as the Han majority. As far as we know, this is the first comprehensive survey of ethnic and national identities ever conducted in China. The survey adopts many questions from the 2003 National Identity Survey conducted by the International Social Survey Programme in 36 countries and regions (but not in China), and allows for a quantitative comparison of China with other countries and regions for the first time. In addition, we use the 2008 China Survey, which was based on a national random sample and jointly conducted by American and Chinese researchers. This national survey helps us further compare Chinese national identity with that in the United States and Russia.

The findings show that ethnic minorities in China expressed strong feelings of intragroup identity through ethnic-language learning, religious practices, and exclusively ethnic-based marriages. Further, Chinese ethnic minorities showed higher levels of both perceived ethnic identity and perceived national identity than their counterparts in the United States and Russia. These findings seem to support the hypothesis of national identity based on the multiethnic Chinese state. We conclude that ethnic relations in China are based on a pact between the government and the ethnic minorities, which requires the government to grant ethnic separation and autonomy while the minorities, in turn, demonstrate their loyalty to the Chinese nation-state. If the state fails to provide the promised autonomy, or the minorities fail to prove their nationalism, the deal may collapse. This study offers a rare empirical perspective to the delicate balance Beijing must maintain to preserve its legitimacy.

Selected Religious and Linguistic Minorities in China

★ Beijing

5

1

3

4

2

1: Xinjiang Autonomous Region: Uyghur
2: Tibet Autonomous Region: Tibetan
3: Inner Mongolia Autonomous Region: Mongol
4: Ningxia Autonomous Region: Hui
5: Yining, Capital of Ili Kazak Autonomous Prefecture

Separate but Loyal:
Ethnicity and
Nationalism in China

Introduction

The single largest ethnic group in China is the Han, which comprises 92 percent of the country's population. This high percentage, however, disguises the complexities of ethnic relations in China. Although most of the 55 officially recognized ethnic minority groups are well integrated and see little difference between themselves and the Han majority, several other groups, such as the Uyghurs, the Tibetans, the Huis, the Mongols, and the Kazaks, have posed serious challenges to the Chinese state's ability to maintain ethnic harmony. Each with millions of people, these groups are difficult to integrate due to their religious and linguistic distinctiveness. They hold important political bargaining power with the state by possessing huge territories and natural resources and by serving as the strategic buffer zones for China's land security in the north, west, and south. In recent years, China's often harsh policy toward the ethnic separatist movements in these regions has been under attack by Western media and governments for human rights violations. The pressure of international public opinion constantly puts China on the defensive and creates damage

Ethnic relations and national identity are burning issues for China's leaders and can potentially shake the Communist Party's legitimacy, regime stability, effective governance, national sovereignty, and territorial integrity.

to its public image. All these complexities make ethnic relations and national identity burning issues for China's leaders. These issues can potentially shake the Communist Party's legitimacy, regime stability, effective governance, national sovereignty, and territorial integrity.

The goal of this study is to examine the relationship between ethnic identity and national identity among China's ethnic groups, particularly among the above-mentioned religiously and linguistically distinctive groups, and to examine the extent to which these groups are assimilated into mainstream Chinese culture. There are four possible outcomes of ethnic and national identities in a given society, depending on the specific political and policy environment (table 1): 1) weak ethnic identity and weak national identity, implying a possibly coerced ethnic integration, but some degree of political stability due to the lack of desire for ethnic independence; 2) weak ethnic identity and strong national identity, suggesting successful integration and political stability due to the desire to stay together; 3) strong ethnic identity and weak national identity, most likely a result of failed integration and a condition for political instability, as shown by the examples of failed states; and, finally, 4) strong ethnic identity and strong national identity, implying successful but unstable ethnic integration and a delicate balance between group equality and national unity. Identifying the specific combination of ethnic and national identities among the religious minorities in China will obviously have important policy implications in how to handle ethnic relations and avoid tension and conflict in the future.

Table 1. Hypothetical Outcomes of Ethnic Policy

	Weak Ethnic Identity	**Strong Ethnic Identity**
Weak National Identity	Coerced integration (stable)	Failed integration (unstable)
Strong National Identity	Successful integration (stable)	Conditional integration (unstable)

Ethnic relations in China are the combined result of complex historical interactions among various ethnic groups and the ethnic policy under the current Communist government. The following section will

discuss the historical patterns of ethnic interaction and the current ethnic policy environment in the People's Republic of China.

Identity Formation in Modern China

Ethnic and national identities in China are shaped by several factors, including the legacy of the Qing empire (1644–1911), the socialist period
from 1949 to 1978, and the post-Mao market reforms since 1978.

The debate among historians about the formation of Chinese
civilization provides valuable insights into contemporary concepts
of Chinese nationalism and ethnic identity. Relying primarily on
Chinese-language sources of historical records, scholars such as Liang
Qichao in the late nineteenth century and early twentieth century argued that Han culture was the driving force of Chinese civilization, which in turn shaped the development of all of Asia (Dikötter 1992). At the core of Chinese culture lies Confucianism, which emphasizes "cultural universalism" rather than ethnic distinction (Dow 1982). This cultural universalism served as a powerful mechanism to absorb any for-
eign forces. Consequently, foreign conquerors such as the Manchus
were sinicized and, as a result, ruled China with Chinese values and
practices (Ho 1967).

Using newly available Qing imperial archives, one scholar argues that the Manchus ruled the Hans by incorporating the Chinese language, Confucian values, and the Han bureaucratic structure, but were by no means sinicized in their dealings with other ethnic groups.

In a thought-provoking article, Rawski (1996) disputes the sinicization thesis by using newly available Manchu-language Qing imperial
archives. According to this view, the Qing expansion in the seventeenth
and eighteenth centuries resulted in a territory that was more than
double the size of the previous Ming dynasty (1368–1644) territory.
The Han population was merely one component of the vast Qing empire, together with the Manchus, Mongols, Tibetans, Uyghurs, Huis,
Kazaks, and others. While the Manchus ruled the Hans by incorporating

the Chinese language, Confucian values, and the Han bureaucratic structure, they were by no means sinicized in their dealings with other ethnic groups. The Qing government set up a banner system of military officials to supervise the Han bureaucracy in China proper. The Council of Colonial Affairs (理藩院) was established to watch over the Inner Asian periphery. It was staffed exclusively by professional soldiers (bannermen), and its documents were in Mongolian, Tibetan, and Manchu. (Rawski 1996; Chia 1993; Zhao 1995).

The Qing rulers used different methods to deal with the various non-Han groups. They claimed common ancestry with the Mongols as a means to form a common ethnic identity (Rawski 1991 and 1996; Hua 1983). They adopted Tibetan Buddhism and invited Buddhist monks to be their spiritual tutors in order to gain their trust (Rawski 1996). Tibetan Buddhism also became a vehicle to strengthen Qing control in Mongolia (Rawski 1996; Zhang 1988). In Xinjiang, the Qing rulers used Chinese-speaking Hui Muslims to fight against the Turkic-speaking Muslims (Rawski 1996; He and Wang 1989; Togan 1992).

In addition, Chinese was not the only official language. From the onset, Manchu was the second language for state documents in the Qing dynasty. Emperor Qianlong claimed to be the ruler of five peoples—Manchus, Mongols, Muslims, Tibetans, and Hans—and announced that their languages were all official languages of the Qing empire (Rawski 1996; Crossley 1985; Jin 1992). The Qing rulers encouraged ethnic-language publications and compiled multilanguage dictionaries (Rawski 1996). These policies helped to preserve the ethnic boundaries of these groups.

The key to the Qing's success in creating an empire that lasted for several hundred years lay in the empire's ability to keep these groups ethnically separate but loyal, and to incorporate group-specific approaches to dealing with different ethnic entities (Rawski 1996 and 2001).

After the Nationalists overthrew the Qing in 1911, Sun Yat-sen's Republic of China faced a fundamental identity crisis from the very beginning. The Nationalists adopted an ideology of anti-Qing, pro-Han Chinese nationalism (Rawski 1996). This ideology put the Mongols, Tibetans, Uyghurs, and Manchus in an interesting position. If they wanted to remain part of China, they could oppose Sun Yat-sen's revolution and support the continued rule of the Qing. However, if the minority groups supported the revolution, then that decision would eventually lead them to break away from what the Nationalists had defined as a Han-centered nation-state. This fundamental flaw in the Nationalist ideology led to the near disintegration of Qing China. Outer Mongolia became permanently independent. Tibet was left virtually unattended from 1911 to 1951. The Uyghurs and Manchus succeeded in gaining temporary independence in the 1930s and 1940s.

The debate among historians about the relationship between the Qing empire and Han culture is a refreshing reminder that current ethnic relations and national identity in China have to be examined not only in light of Han civilization, but also, perhaps more importantly, through the lens of the Qing legacies, which were not exclusively derived from Confucian thinking.

Intentionally or not, the Chinese Communists were able to avoid this flaw in the Nationalist ideology. The Communists adopted an ideology that emphasized class distinction rather than ethnic distinction. China's nationalism was not defined as against the Manchus (thanks to the Nationalist success in overthrowing them), but, instead, against Western imperialists. The Communist interpretation of nationalism, therefore, did not contradict ethnic coexistence within the original Qing framework. This fact,

China's official policy states that all 56 ethnic groups are equal. This policy of ethnic equality is implemented through state-sponsored affirmative action programs.

combined with force when deemed necessary, is probably one reason the Communists succeeded in keeping most of the Qing territories under their control.

Currently, the Chinese official policy on ethnicity states that all 56 ethnic groups (55 minorities plus Han) are equal.[1] Each has the right and freedom to use its own spoken and written language and to preserve its own way of life. Regional autonomy is practiced in areas where ethnic minorities are concentrated, though any effort to instigate secession is strictly prohibited.[2]

This policy of ethnic equality is implemented through state-sponsored affirmative action programs. A quota system was set up to ensure access to education,[3] employment, and urban housing, and to promote holding public office (He 2006). Taxation is reduced in less developed minority regions. Family planning designed to restrict population growth is enforced more strictly among the Han majority than among minorities, resulting in higher growth rates among minority populations in recent years.[4] Similar to Qing policies, ethnic-language publications and broadcasts continue to flourish (Gladney 1998; Mackerras 2004a; Rossabi 2004), and bilingual education is encouraged (Postiglione, Jiao, and Gyatso 2005; Teng 2005; Zhou 2000).

It would be naïve to evaluate ethnic relations based only on this rosy picture. People are constantly reminded of the repressive nature of the Communist regime against minorities and the regime's efforts to assimilate them. It is undeniable that the Chinese government has suppressed numerous instances of unrest by minorities; however, it has also resolutely suppressed Han majority unrest, particularly those instances that threatened the fundamental legitimacy of the Communist Party (Sichuan Research Group 2001). That said, additional evidence is needed to show whether China is indeed more repressive against minorities than against the majority. Regarding Chinese assimilation of minorities, the Han economic expansion into minority regions has no doubt negatively impacted minority cultures and altered their life-

Chinese identity has been described as an 'imagined community,' in which all ethnic groups, big or small, are inalienable and equal.

style. Yet, at the same time, the Han Chinese are themselves the product of global assimilation. They did not invent computers, cell phones, cars, highways, skyscrapers, rock and roll, and the golden arches; instead, they simply facilitated the introduction of these things to minority areas. If Chinese assimilation is equated with the promotion of Chinese nationalism, the evidence to that effect is well documented by researchers (Gries 2004a and 2004b). But, according to official policy, Chinese nationalism is not the same thing as Han nationalism. In the official constitutional framework, the Hans are merely one of the 56 ethnic groups. Chinese identity is, hence, an "imagined community" (Anderson 1991) in which all ethnic groups, big or small, are inalienable and equal.

The market reforms that began in the late 1970s have changed the lives of many ethnic minorities. Political decentralization aimed at creating more local economic incentives has resulted in more power and control by local ethnic officials. Increased investment and economic aid from the more-developed regions of China have led to improved living standards and better education among minorities (Wang 2004; Mackerras 2004b). Market reforms have commercialized minority cultures and resulted in ethnic films, pop singers, theme parks, restaurants, etc. These aspects of political and economic modernization have, ironically, made both the Hans and the minorities more aware of what separates them. There has been more religious freedom for minority groups as well. For example, Chinese Muslim delegations have been allowed to travel abroad, and Chinese Islamic schools have sent students to Egypt, Libya, and Pakistan. From 1984 to 2001, some 30,000 Muslims in Xinjiang visited Mecca (Xinjiang Research Group 2001). Chinese Muslims have also gained more opportunities to interact with Muslims abroad through expanded trade and tourism (Gladney 1998; Mackerras 2004a; Rossabi 2004; Kapstein 2006).

Market reforms have not always been beneficial to ethnic relations. One negative effect has been the increased Han migration into minority regions such as Xinjiang and Tibet, which has led to competition for jobs with the local people. A freer labor market, while necessary for economic efficiency, has created further income and status gaps and rising tensions between Han migrants and local minorities (Ma et al. 2005; Ma and Dunzengluzhu 2006; Xinjiang Research Group 2001). Finally, improved living standards and education that resulted from the reforms have given minorities more time and knowledge to evaluate their political rights. Decades of affirmative action policies have made the minorities more group conscious. They are "coming out" and becoming more assertive (Gladney 2004b), emulating a similar pattern that emerged in the post-Brezhnev Soviet Union (Karklins 1987).

Meanwhile, market reform and political decentralization have led to a decline in traditional communist ideology. Nationalism has become an alternative source of political mobilization (Tang 2005). Consequently, there was a surge of Chinese nationalism in the 1990s, which continued to grow in the 2000s. The Communist Party has been only partially successful in keeping popular nationalism under control, and, at times, the state has been compelled to satisfy the public's nationalist sentiment (Gries 2004a and 2004b). Thus, Chinese nationalism is growing side by side with ethnic identity. What is unclear, however, is whether the growing sentiment of Chinese nationalism is only a Han phenomenon, or if it is also shared among minorities.

The Religious Minorities in China

This study focuses on five ethnic minorities—Uyghur, Tibetan, Mongol, Hui, and Kazak—while the Han majority is used as a comparison group. These groups have been selected because of their geographic significance (except for the geographically dispersed Hui) and, more importantly, because they are religious groups. These religious groups share all-encompassing belief systems that may be incompatible with the official ideologies of communism and Chinese nationalism. Their leaders are capable of mobilizing resources and organizing collective resistance, and even independence, within their communities and across regions and national boundaries (Shih, Liu, and Zhang 2007). Scholars have spent their entire careers studying these groups. Rather than presenting an authoritative discussion of the history, culture, and internal variation of these groups, we will only focus on describing the general background of each and exploring its relationship with China.

> *These religious groups share all-encompassing belief systems that may be incompatible with the official ideologies of communism and Chinese nationalism.*

Uyghurs

Among China's 55 officially recognized minority groups, the Uyghurs are the fifth largest, with a population of 8.4 million in the 2000 census (State Statistics Bureau 2001). The Uyghurs are Sunni Muslims and speak Uyghur, which belongs to the Altaic-Turkic language family. Most Uyghurs live in Xinjiang Autonomous Region in northwest China. Although Xinjiang has a small manufacturing base, it ranks the highest in per capita income among the inland provinces due to its natural resources and agricultural production (Wiemer 2004), and the region's illiteracy rate is a relatively low 8.8 percent (State Statistics Bureau 2001).

In 1765, the Qing empire first defeated and then united the kingdoms in the northwestern region. Subsequently, the Qing ruled the region indirectly through the native elites (Millward 1998; Chia 1993), a pattern that was also typical in Mongolia and Tibet. In 1884, the Qing declared the region a province and named it Xinjiang ("new territory" in Chinese). Xinjiang is China's largest region, equalling three times the size of France and occupying one-sixth of China's total territory (Millward and Perdue 2004a and 2004b). It shares borders with eight countries (Mongolia, Russia, Kazakhstan, Kyrgyzstan, Tajikistan, Pakistan, Afghanistan, and India) and serves as China's strategic route to Central Asia.

Since the Qing conquest in the mid-eighteenth century, the Uyghurs have launched numerous independence movements. In 1864, they founded the Kingdom of Kashgaria, which was later suppressed by the Qing general Zuo Zongtang. In 1933, when the Nationalist government was distracted by the Japanese invasion of northeastern China, the Uyghurs set up the Islamic Eastern Turkestan Republic, which was ultimately overthrown by the Nationalists in 1934. From 1944 to 1949, when the Nationalists and the Communists were busy fighting each other, the Uyghurs again declared independence.

> *Xinjiang is China's largest region, equalling three times the size of France and occupying one-sixth of China's total territory.*

This, too, was later suppressed by the Communists (Fuller and Lipman 2004). The collapse of the Soviet Union in the late 1980s led to the independence of the Central Asian republics (Kazakhstan, Kyrgyzstan, Tajikistan, and Uzbekistan). These events along China's borders inspired another wave of uprisings led by the East Turkistan Independence Movement,[5] such as the 1990 Baren uprising near Kashgar; the 1992 bombings in Yining, Urumqi, and Kashgar; the 1997 bus bombing in Urumqi; the 1995 Khotan demonstration; the 1996 assassinations of Uyghur officials in Kucha, Kashgar, and Aksu; the 1997 Yining demonstration in northern Xinjiang (Millward 2004); and the 2009 Uyghur riot in Urumqi, resulting in nearly 200 people killed (mostly Hans), as reported by the state-controlled media (Wong 2009).[6] In response to these events, China declared the East Turkistan Independence Movement a terrorist group. In addition to keeping an iron grip in Xinjiang, China in recent years has also stepped up its economic aid and continued Han settlement in the region (Backman 2004).

For most of the past 250 years, China has managed to keep Xinjiang under its control. While some authors have reported widespread discontent with Chinese rule among Uyghurs due to the state's effort to strengthen their Chinese identity and weaken their Uyghur identity (Bovingdon 2004a, 2004b, and 2004c; Dwyer 2005; Teague 2009), others have found it to be a relatively calm relationship. A 2000 survey conducted by researchers at Xinjiang Normal University found that more than 80 percent of Uyghur respondents supported the government's crackdown on ethnic separatism and illegal religious activities (Yao and Ma 2005: 39). One author found that most of the uprisings were small in scale and that Xinjiang did not pose a serious security threat to China (Millward 2004).

Tibetans

With a population of 5.4 million in the 2000 census, Tibetans are the ninth largest group in China. About 46 percent of them live in the Tibet Autonomous Region (TAR), and the rest in the neighboring Chinese provinces of Qinghai, Sichuan, Gansu, and Yunnan. Located in the southwestern corner of China, the TAR shares international borders with India, Bhutan, Nepal, and Myanmar and is the second-largest provincial-level entity next to Xinjiang.

The Tibetan plateau is one of the most isolated places in the world—and one of the poorest regions in China.

With an average elevation of 4,500 meters, or almost 15,000 feet, and surrounded by the Himalaya Mountains, the Tibetan plateau is one of the most isolated places in the world. Tibet is also one of the poorest regions in China, with an illiteracy rate of 45.5 percent, according to the 2000 population census, and a per capita disposable income ranked at the bottom of 31 provincial units in 2006 (State Statistics Bureau 2001 and 2007). After Buddhism migrated to Tibet two thousand years ago, it virtually disappeared from its birthplace in India. Thanks to the Fourteenth Dalai Lama's public relations efforts, Tibet is known around the world as the center of Buddhism. Tibetan is categorized as one of the Tibeto-

Burman languages, and its writing system is based on a branch of classical Indian Sanskrit.

In the 1720s, the Qing armies defeated the Zunghars and took control of Tibet. The Qing empire claimed suzerainty over Tibet, set up military garrisons, and established the Office of the Governor (*amban*). It left the management of Tibet's internal affairs mostly to the Tibetans. This system of laissez-faire control lasted until 1911, when the Qing empire was overthrown by the Nationalist government led by Sun Yat-sen. From 1911 to 1951, the Nationalists were preoccupied with internal political instabilities and Japanese invasion. During this period, Tibet exercised *de facto* independence, while the Nationalist government continued to claim suzerainty over the region.[7] In 1951, two years after Mao Zedong defeated Chiang Kai-shek's Nationalist government, the Communist government in Beijing signed a treaty with the Fourteenth Dalai Lama's delegates, granting Tibet's sovereignty to China, but its internal autonomy to the Tibetan government. In 1959, Mao's radical socialist land-reform policies threatened this delicate balance of combined rule. The policies put pressure on the Tibetan government's religion-based legitimacy, polarizing opposition to Chinese rule. As a result of this and with the help of the U.S. government, the Fourteenth Dalai Lama staged an armed uprising against China, which was quickly suppressed by Communist troops. The Dalai Lama, along with 100,000-plus followers, fled to Dharamsala in northern India and set up the Government of Tibet in Exile.[8] The Fourteenth Dalai Lama advocated Tibetan independence until the

Mao's radical socialist land-reform policies threatened the legitimacy of Tibet's unity of religion and the state and provoked opposition to Chinese rule by the local religious-political elite. The campaign led by Western human rights groups to boycott the 2008 Beijing Olympics provoked strong public resentment and the rise of nationalism both inside China and among the overseas Chinese communities.

late 1980s, when he agreed to recognize Chinese sovereignty in Tibet, though he continued to demand greater Tibetan autonomy under Chinese rule.

With strong support and encouragement from the Government of Tibet in Exile, international human rights groups, and the Western media, Tibetans in China organized several violent protests against Chinese rule in the 1980s and 1990s. China's response was to declare martial law in Tibet, while continuing to appease the Tibetan population with increased economic aid.[9] In March 2008, violent Tibetan protests and riots broke out again in an apparent attempt to express Tibetan resentment of Han immigration into Tibet. The subsequent crackdown on the riots led to a campaign by many Western human rights groups to boycott the 2008 Beijing Olympics (Greenberg 2008). This campaign provoked strong Chinese public resentment and the rise of nationalism both inside the country and among the overseas Chinese communities.

Mongols

Mongols are China's eighth largest ethnic group, with a population of 5.8 million in 2000.[10] Some Mongols live in northern Xinjiang, but most live in the Inner Mongolia Autonomous Region located in northern and northeastern parts of China. Inner Mongolia Autonomous Region is the third largest among China's 31 provincial administrative units. Inner Mongolia, Xinjiang, and Tibet together form more than 42 percent of China's total territory. Similar to Xinjiang and Tibet, Mongolia (including both inner and outer Mongolias) was conquered by the Qing empire in 1757, when the Manchus defeated the Zunghars. In 1921, Outer Mongolia (Mongolian People's Republic) declared independence during a period of political turmoil in China, while Inner Mongolia Autonomous Region remained a part of China. The Nationalist government refused to recognize Outer Mongolia's independence and continued to include it in its map of China. Similar to Uyghur, Mongolian is one of the Altaic languages. Its writing system is based on a vertical form of Sanskrit, which is still used in Inner Mongolia. The Mongolian People's Republic (Outer Mongolia), heavily influenced by Russia, replaced its writing system with the Cyrillic alphabet. Tibetan Buddhism was introduced to Mongolia during the Qing period.

Beginning in the Qing empire, China encouraged population migration into Inner Mongolia as well as Xinjiang. In the 2000 population census, the Han population made up 80 percent of Inner Mongolia, as compared to just over 40 percent in Xinjiang and only 6 percent in Tibet. In spite of the Han domination in their native land, Mongols share a sense of superiority over the Han people. Unlike their ethnic minority counterparts in Xinjiang and Tibet, Mongols conquered and ruled the Han people for 100 years from the thirteenth to the fourteenth centuries under the Mongol empire. In the mind of the Hans, the Mongol empire was simply called Yuan, which is one of

In spite of Han domination in their native land, Mongols share a sense of superiority over the Han people.

the Chinese dynasties that was sinicized by Han culture. For Mongols, however, the Han people were the subjects of Kublai Khan, and China was part of the Mongol empire. This historical pride is openly and prominently displayed by the numerous Genghis Khan statues and portraits in museums, schools, and other public spaces in both Inner Mongolia and the Mongolian People's Republic. Mongols in China enjoy a relatively high level of education. The illiteracy rate among Mongols is 7.2 percent, slightly lower than the 7.3 percent among Hans (8.8 percent for Uyghur and 45.5 percent for Tibetans). Inner Mongolia's economy is also more developed than Xinjiang and Tibet. In 2006, its per capita disposable income ranked twelfth in the country (State Statistics Bureau 2001 and 2007).

After an unsuccessful attempt to reunify with Outer Mongolia in 1911, ethnic nationalism took an interesting turn in Inner Mongolia. In the 1930s and 1940s, Mongol nationalists fought the Nationalist government in order to gain more autonomy. Their goal was to move away from provincial administrative status under Nationalist control and become an autonomous region (Bulag 2004). The Communist Party saw Mongol aspirations for autonomy as a lever against Nationalist rule, and took advantage of this opportunity by supporting Inner Mongolian nationalists. Subsequently, the Communist Party made an alliance with the Inner Mongolian nationalist movement. In 1947, two years before the Communists drove the Nationalists to Taiwan,

Inner Mongolian nationalists founded the Inner Mongolia Autonomous Region, which covered several provinces under Nationalist control (热河, 察哈尔, 绥远). The Communist leaders supported this movement in an effort to weaken that control. After 1949, Inner Mongolia maintained its status as an autonomous region, while staying within the framework of the People's Republic of China.

However, Inner Mongolia has not been free from ethnic tension. In the 1960s, when China and the Soviet Union were locked in a cold war, Mao purged a large number of former members of the Inner Mongolian People's Party, which had been founded in 1925 with Soviet support. This tactic alienated some Inner Mongolians (Bulag 2004). In the 1980s and 1990s, Chinese authorities arrested and jailed Inner Mongolian student activists who opposed increasing Han Chinese influence in Inner Mongolia. In 1997, some of these former student activists from Inner Mongolia University founded the overseas Inner Mongolian People's Party. Its goal is to overthrow Chinese rule.[11] Despite all these incidents, researchers and reporters seem to agree that the overall ethnic tension in Inner Mongolia is far less than in Xinjiang and Tibet (Bulag 2004; Burjgin and Bilik 2003; Wang 2003; Reuters 2000).

Huis

The Huis are Sufi Muslims and the third largest minority after the Zhuangs and the Manchus, with a population of 9.8 million in the 2000 census (State Statistics Bureau 2001). Unlike the Uyghurs, Tibetans, Mongols, and Kazaks, the Huis are not territory-based, but are the most scattered ethnic group in China. Most of them live in northwestern China (Ningxia Hui Autonomous Region, Qinghai, Gansu, and Xinjiang), while many other Huis can be found in Henan, Hebei, Shandong, Anhui, and other provinces, as well as in the cities of Beijing and Tianjin. The common tie that binds the Huis is Islam, as well as their collective identity as descendants of Arab and Persian merchants who

> ***Unlike the Uyghurs, Tibetans, Mongols, and Kazaks, the Huis are not territory-based, but are, rather, the most scattered ethnic group in China.***

first came to China in the seventh century and later in the thirteenth century (Lipman 1997 and 2004). The Huis do not have their own language, and the majority speak Mandarin. Although most neither speak nor understand Arabic or Persian, there is increasingly a desire to learn these languages and, thus, be more authentically Hui (Lipman 2004). Arabic used to be taught in Hui schools in the 1910s, and renewed interest in learning Arabic has been growing since the 1980s (Jin 2007). The Huis are better educated (15.6 percent illiteracy) than the Tibetans, but less so than the Mongols and the Uyghurs (State Statistics Bureau 2001).

Although the Huis are more integrated into Chinese society than the Uyghurs, the Tibetans, the Mongols, and the Kazaks, this integration does not guarantee harmony. They rebelled against the Qing empire in the mid-nineteenth century and against the Nationalist government after the Qing was overthrown. Under Communist rule, there have been a number of protests and clashes involving the Huis due to their mistreatment by the Hans. In the early 1970s, radical Maoists forced Huis in Shadian, Yunnan, to raise pigs and eat pork, which created strong resentment (Lipman 2004 and Gladney 1991). In 1990, a street fight between some Huis and Hans near Kunming re-

> *The Huis have coexisted with the Hans for the past 1,300 years, but they are far from being invisible on China's radar screen of ethnic conflict. One author vividly described them as 'familiar strangers.'*

sulted in the police opening fire and killing three Hui Muslims. In 1993, Hui Muslims protested against a Chinese newspaper's insult to Islam and Muslims in Xining, Qinghai. In 2000, Hui protests broke out in Yangxin, Shandong, when a Han shop owner advertised his pork as "Muslim pork," trying to portray it as *halal* food, despite the Muslim prohibition of pork (Lipman 2004). In 2004, a major violent confrontation broke out between the Huis and the Hans in Henan, after a Hui taxi driver fatally hit a Han girl and Hans retaliated by nailing a pig head on the gate of the local mosque. The fight left 150 dead (Kahn 2004; Yardley 2006). The Huis have coexisted with the Hans for the past 1,300 years, but they are far from being invisible on

China's radar screen of ethnic conflict. One author vividly described them as "familiar strangers" (Lipman 1997).

Kazaks

The Kazaks are another Muslim group. Their population of 1.1 million makes them the fifteenth largest of the 55 minorities. Most of the Kazaks live in northern Xinjiang's Ili Kazak Autonomous Prefecture, Barkol Kazak Autonomous County, and Mori Kazak Autonomous County. The rest live in Gansu and Qinghai. Historically, the Kazaks migrated to their current location from the Altai Mountains. They officially became part of Xinjiang under the Qing empire. Most Kazaks only speak their own language, which is part of the Altay language family. Their nomadic lifestyle makes education difficult, yet the 2000 population census reported a surprisingly low illiteracy rate of 3.2 percent (State Statistics Bureau 2001). Because the Kazaks are geographically separated from the Hans, there have been few known clashes between these groups. The more immediate concern for the Kazaks is, instead, their relations with the nearby Uyghurs and Huis (Gladney 1996).

The 2006–2007 Chinese Ethnicity Surveys

The primary source of information for this study is based on the 2006–2007 Chinese Ethnicity Surveys conducted by these authors. The surveys were conducted in Tibet (2006) and Xinjiang (2007) and included 1,598 students in 17 public high schools. In each school, classes were selected based on grade level, ethnic composition, and language of instruction. Questionnaires in Uyghur, Tibetan, and Chinese (depending on the language of instruction) were distributed to all students in the 34 selected classes. Trained research team members assured the respondents of the confidentiality of their answers, explained the questionnaire, answered the respondents' questions, and collected the completed questionnaires. The stratified nonprobability sample was designed to represent several key aspects that may affect

The 2006–2007 Chinese Ethnicity Surveys were conducted in Tibet and Xinjiang among 1,598 students in 17 public high schools.

ethnic identity. The sample includes adequate numbers of respondents from six key ethnic groups: Uyghur, Tibetan, Kazak, Hui, Mongol, and Han. The five minority groups were chosen because of their religious and linguistic distinction from the Han group. As discussed earlier, these groups are China's "religious minorities." They draw special attention from the Communist Party due to their ability to organize collective resistance (Shih, Liu, and Zhang 2007). Another characteristic of the sample is its representation of regions with a diverse range of social and economic conditions and various degrees of ethnic integration, including: Lhasa, Nyingchi, Shigatse, Gyangse, and Shannan in Tibet and Urumqi, Turpan, Ili, Changji, Shihezi, and Yecheng in Xinjiang. The selected schools and classes in the sample are also representative of the gender ratio, school grades (seventh grade to twelfth grade), ethnic composition, and language of instruction (Mandarin only, mixed, and ethnic-language only—See appendices 1 and 2).

Ethnic relations are a sensitive topic in China. Special attention is required to decide what questions can be asked in order to reveal as accurately as possible the true feelings of the respondents. If the question is too direct, fear of political incorrectness may make the respondent hide his/her real answer. For example, a 2001 survey on ethnic relations in Xinjiang (Yee 2005) asked the respondents whether they agreed with the statement that Xinjiang was a part of China, which elicited an overwhelmingly high percentage of affirmative answers. Such findings, how-

> *Ethnic relations are a sensitive topic in China. If questions are too direct, fear of political incorrectness may make respondents hide their real answers.*

ever, may not be reliable since the respondents may have feared that a "no" answer could be labeled as treason. To avoid skewed results, we purposely designed three groups of indirect questions to measure ethnic identity and national identity. The questions gathered information on the students' motivation to learn their own languages and the reasons underlying that motivation, their attitudes toward interethnic marriage, and their religious values and practices. Although religious practice is a far less sensitive topic than the direct political question mentioned earlier, nonetheless, it is still a touchy topic given the government's ban on religion in China's public schools. If the reported level of religious practice in the sample is low, it may not reflect the reality and, therefore, the question may be flawed. On the other hand, if the degree of reported religious practice is high, it may be an indication that the question worked and the respondents were not afraid of telling the truth.

In addition to the three groups of questions on language study, interethnic marriage, and religion, we also adapted several questions from the 2003 National Identity Survey (II), which was conducted by the International Social Survey Programme in 36 countries and regions, but not in China.[12] Examples of these questions included the respondent's feelings of closeness toward his/her country, and toward his/her own ethnic group. These questions add more values to the Chinese Ethnicity Surveys by making it possible to compare ethnic and national identities in China with those in other countries.

Admittedly, our sample does not represent the adult ethnic population, whose attitudes may differ from those of high-school students. Yet a look at these high-school students may provide more understanding of the political socialization process which they are going through, and, hence, shed light on future trends of ethnic identity among these groups.

Another limitation of the surveys is that they do not include probability subsamples of the six ethnic groups. For example, the Han students were not a random sample of the entire Han student population in China, but were drawn only from Tibet and Xinjiang. This limitation can be overcome by comparing the differences among the six groups, rather than focusing on the variation within a single group, while taking into consideration other factors that may influence ethnic identity, such as gender, family income, school year, parental ethnic origin, exposure to ethnic integration, and political mobilization. This multifactor approach can avoid the limitation of a nonprobability sample (Manion 1994 and 2010).

Another potential problem of our sample is that the Mongol students were actually residents in the Kazak region in northern Xinjiang. These Mongol students may be less integrated with the Hans than the Mongols living in Inner Mongolia, where there is more Han influence. There may be a problem if the Mongol students in the sample demonstrate as little sinicization as the Kazaks, since the Mongols in Inner Mongolia are perhaps more sinicized than the Kazaks. On the other hand, the sample may be representative if the Mongol students show more integration with Han culture than the Kazaks and the Uyghurs.

Below, we will examine ethnic identity through three measures, namely, language learning, interethnic marriage, and religious practice. Then, we will compare China with the United States and Russia in terms of ethnic and national identities, and assess the consequences of China's ethnic policy.

Language and Identity

The importance of language in forging group identity is well documented. A common language transmits common ideas and serves to define the boundary of a group (Hu 2008; Zhu 2007; Gao 2006; Schiaffini 2004; Barrington 2002; Laitin 2000; Kolas 1996; Nash 1996; Williams 1984; Issacs 1975).

Except during the radical Cultural Revolution in the 1960s and 1970s, bilingual education has been the official language policy (Zhou 2000 and 2004, Teng 2005). The 1995 Education Law states that the Han language is the basic language of instruction. Ethnic minority schools can use their own language as the teaching language, but they are required to teach Mandarin at some point before the seventh grade.[13]

Some researchers, however, argue that the rhetoric of bilingual education is based on half-truths, and that China's covert policy is, in fact, monolingualism (Teague 2009). Citing quotes from the U.S. Congress–funded Radio Free Asia and local Communist Party officials' speeches, Dwyer (2005) warns that this covert monolingual policy has shaped Uyghur life in Xinjiang in the past 20 years (p. 34). Uyghur students are required to take Chinese in first grade (p. 38), and Chinese has been the language of instruction since the mid-1990s (p. 39). This picture is quite different from our own visit to a school outside Kashgar in Xinjiang in

> *Except during the radical Cultural Revolution, bilingual education has been the official language policy. Some researchers argue, however, that China's covert policy is monolingualism.*

2005, and another school in Tingri, Tibet, in 2006, where the languages of instruction were exclusively Uyghur and Tibetan, with Chinese only required as a foreign language after third grade (also see Benson 2004). Minority students still have the option to take the annual college entrance exam in their own language (Clothey 2005). These anecdotal examples, admittedly, may not reflect the entire situation, which should be further examined with more empirical evidence.

Sometimes language policy reflects bureaucratic turf wars, and discrepancies in policy outcomes arise between local and central governments and between different bureaucratic agencies in Beijing. For example, the Ministry of Education is in favor of Mandarin education, but the State Ethnic Affairs Council supports the use of ethnic languages.[14] A comparison of the 1995 Education Law (Article 12, described above) and the 2004

> *Sometimes language policy reflects bureaucratic turf wars, and discrepancies arise between local and central governments and between different bureaucratic agencies in Beijing.*

revised Law on Regional National Autonomy (Article 37)[15] shows such a discrepancy. According to the Education Law, ethnic schools "可以" (can but don't have to) use ethnic languages, but Mandarin is the basic teaching language. The Law on Regional National Autonomy states that ethnic schools "应当" (should be encouraged to) use ethnic language as the teaching language. Clearly, there is a discrepancy between unity and diversity based on opposing bureaucratic interests. It is unclear, however, which side has the upper hand.

In order to answer this question, we asked in the surveys when the student began learning math in Mandarin. This question served as a measure of Chinese-language exposure. The highest exposure is from preschool and the lowest is zero (still using ethnic language). We calculated the average levels of Chinese-language exposure among Han, Hui, Mongol, Tibetan, Uyghur, and Kazak students, while controlling for school year (figure 1). The findings show significant gaps between these groups. Using Han students' Mandarin exposure as 100 percent, Huis (99 percent) and Mongols (98 percent) were just about

Figure 1. Chinese-Language Exposure by Ethnicity

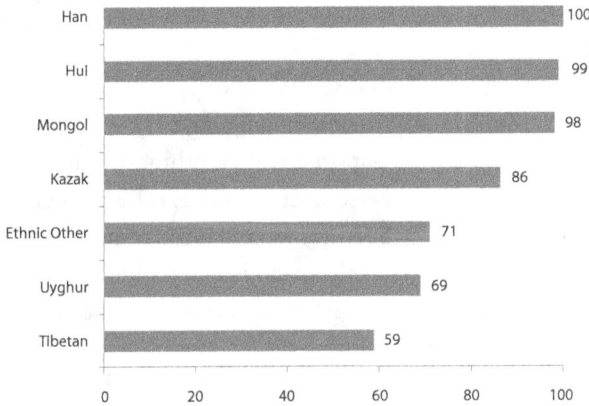

Source: 2006–2007 Chinese Ethnicity Surveys
Note: Chinese-language exposure is based on when the respondent began to learn math with Chinese as the language of instruction. The earliest (preschool) is coded 1, while no exposure (still using ethnic language in math class) is coded 0. Other grades (first grade thru senior high) when the respondents began to use Chinese as the language of instruction are coded between 1 and 0. The percentages are derived from an OLS regression analysis using Chinese-language exposure as the dependent variable and ethnicity as the independent variable. All OLS coefficients compare with Han students' exposure. For example, the OLS coefficient for Tibetan students is -.41, indicating that Tibetan students' exposure is 41 percent less than Han students. If Han students' exposure is 100 percent, Tibetan students' is 59 percent. Year of schooling is included in the OLS regression equation, but not shown. The differences among Han, Kazak, Ethnic Other, Uyghur, and Tibetan are statistically significant at p<.001. No statistically significant difference is found among Han, Mongol, and Hui.

as equally exposed as Hans. Kazak students were about 14 percent less exposed to Mandarin than Han students, Uyghur students were 31 perrcent less exposed, and the least exposed were Tibetan students (41 percent less than Han students). These findings suggest that if sinicization was measured by Mandarin exposure, it indeed occurred among the Hui and Mongol students. By contrast, bilingual education was implemented among Tibetans, Uyghurs, and, to a lesser degree, Kazaks, with the result that these groups were significantly less sinicized and their own languages were more actively used, at least in school education.

Some researchers argue that ethnic-language education does not prevent sinicization. Although textbooks are written in ethnic languages, their content is sinicized with pro-China patriotic ideas (Bass 2005). Things that are important to ethnic students, such as religion,

are excluded from these ethnic-language textbooks, making them irrelevant to the students' everyday lives. As a result, students lose interest
in education, including learning their own languages (Postiglione et al.
2005; Johnson and Chhetri 2000).

One way to test this hypothesis is to examine the importance ethnic
students attach to learning their own language. If they think that learning their own language is important, then ethnic-language education,
even if sinicized, may not be so irrelevant that it loses its attraction. In
the 2006–2007 Ethnicity Surveys, we asked the respondents about the
relative importance of their ethnic language, Chinese, and English. A
comparison of the three languages may reveal the respondents' sense of
identity to different ethnic entities.

In table 2A, ethnic minority students all attached more importance
(ranging from 10.5 percent to 25.4 percent) to learning their own language than the Han students' reported desire to learn Chinese. For
Hui and Mongol students, learning Chinese was more important than
learning their own language (Arabic or Mongolian). For Tibetan, Uyghur, and Kazak students, learning their ethnic language was more

Table 2. Language Importance and Language for Culture by
Ethnicity (OLS Coefficients)

	A. How Important Is			B. Studying Language for Culture		
	Ethnic	Chinese	English	Ethnic	Chinese	English
Hui	*0.137*	*0.148*	0.075	*0.091*	-0.020	-0.084
Mongol	*0.157*	*0.195*	*0.089*	*0.409*	*-0.232*	*-0.188*
Tibetan	*0.105*	*0.076*	*0.029*	*0.364*	*-0.250*	-0.236
Kazak	*0.151*	*0.071*	*0.065*	*0.327*	*-0.278*	*-0.188*
Uyghur	*0.122*	0.022	*0.020*	*0.290*	*-0.225*	*-0.129*
Ethnic Other	*0.254*	-0.023	0.127	*0.253*	*-0.253*	*-0.014*

Source: 2006–2007 Chinese Ethnicity Surveys

Note: All coefficients compare with Han, p<=.05 if *italic/bold*, p<=.01 if *italic/bold/underline*.
Year of schooling, gender, family income, Chinese-language exposure, membership in the
Communist Youth League, and mixed-parent heritage are included in the OLS analysis,
but not shown. See appendix 1 for further details.

important than learning Chinese. English was the least important for all ethnic groups. These findings suggest that ethnic–language education has not lost its attraction, and that ethnic identity, as measured by language learning, was stronger than Chinese identity, particularly among Tibetan, Uyghur, and Kazak students.

One problem with this conclusion is that the perceived importance of ethnic languages does not necessarily mean it is culturally important. If ethnic languages are instruments for political indoctrination, attaching importance to ethnic languages may still result in sinicization. To solve this problem, we specifically asked the respondents in the surveys whether their desire to study each language was for continuing their respective cultural traditions, including religious traditions. The contrast in table 2B is quite strong. Compared to Han students, minority students across the board were much more likely to learn their own language in order to carry on their cultural heritage. Their reasons for learning Chinese and English, by contrast, were anything but cultural, but reflected, perhaps, the pragmatic purpose of finding a job.

In short, the 2006–2007 surveys show that language sinicization through Chinese-language exposure varied greatly among minority students. The significantly lesser degree of language sinicization among Tibetan and Uyghur students than among Hui and Mongol students indicates that bilingual education was, indeed, the norm for Tibetan and Uyghur students, at least in 2006 and 2007. More interestingly, minority students seemed to be very interested in learning their languages as a way to help them carry on cultural traditions. This is surprising if one believes that the content of ethnic-language education is so sinicized that minority students have no interest in it. The findings in this section show that ethnic identity, when measured by language identity, was significantly stronger among minority students than among Han students, and that such ethnic identity may be a result of bilingual education.

> *Minority students seemed to be very interested in learning their languages as a way to carry on cultural traditions.*

Religion and Identity

Nawang was our Tibetan tour guide when we visited Tibet in 2006. During the many tours of Buddhist monasteries in and around Lhasa, Ganden, Gyangse, Shigatse, Sakya, and Tingri, Nawang's opening line was almost always the same: "This monastery was destroyed during

> *The tour guide's opening line was almost always the same: 'This monastery was destroyed during the Cultural Revolution and rebuilt in the 1980s.'*

the Cultural Revolution and rebuilt in the 1980s." We were sure that he had read our *Lonely Planet Guide to Tibet.* "Why would the same Communist Party that destroyed the monasteries want to rebuild them?" one of the tourists usually asked. Nawang shrugged his shoulders and did not give an answer. At 16, he had gone to Dharamsala

and studied under the Tibetan Government in Exile for 10 years. He spoke fluent English with an Indian accent. Upon his return to Lhasa, he took a job working for a state-owned Chinese tourist company. We asked him why the Chinese trusted him enough to give him this job. He said that his mother worked for the TAR (Tibetan Autonomous Region) government and had good connections there. We were under the impression that Tibet was becoming freer until one day, after watching the monks' daily debate exercises at Sera Monastery, we were invited to a head monk's living quarters. This was a pleasant surprise, and we happily accepted the invitation. Our excitement did not last very long. An ethnic Tibetan police officer working for the local public security bureau showed up as soon as we sat down. He spoke Tibetan to the head monk and asked Nawang to tell us to leave immediately (photo 1).

A similar experience occurred during our visit to Xinjiang in 2005. At the Id Kah Mosque in Kashgar, a huge stone tablet stood near the gate. On it were carvings in Uyghur, Chinese, and English, describing several major renovations funded by the government in 1962, 1983, 1994, and 1999. This led us to believe that religious freedom was flourishing, a notion that quickly burst when we visited the Kashgar Keshan Teacher's School where slogans were posted outside the buildings:

Photo 1. *A Policeman Questioned a Tibetan Monk After Our Visit. Photo by Wenfang Tang, 2006.*

"Oppose separatism! Oppose infiltration!" Inside the main building, there was a huge billboard, taking up an entire wall. It listed seven don'ts in both Chinese and Uyghur (photo 2):

1. Do not propagate religion
2. Do not believe and practice religion
3. Do not wear religious costumes
4. Do not do anything to damage national unity
5. Do not say anything to hurt national unity
6. Do not take part in any separatist activities
7. Do not spread feudal superstition

On the background of the billboard was a picture of modern skyscrapers. The message seemed to be that religion was an impediment to Xinjiang's modernization.

To examine this contrast between religious freedom and state control (also see Barnet 2006), we asked the respondents in the 2006–2007

Photo 2. *A Billboard Banning Religious Practices in Uyghur and Chinese at the Kashgar Keshan Teacher's School. Photo by Wenfang Tang, 2005.*

Ethnicity Surveys whether they believed in any religion. Only about 8 percent of Han students reported that they were Buddhists, and 89 percent did not have any religious affiliation. We were somewhat surprised to find a high degree of religious affiliation among minority students. In spite of the ban on religion in public schools, 63 percent of Tibetan and 88 percent of Mongol respondents declared that they were Buddhists, and 75 percent of Uyghur, 86 percent of Hui, and 95 percent of Kazak respondents reported that they were Muslims. As with many other aspects of Chinese life, the official policy is harsh, yet people routinely find a way around the rules. State officials are well aware of the transgression, but they mostly leave violators alone, as long as they do not threaten national security. The high percentage of reported religious believers is also an indication that the respondents were not afraid of telling the truth. That is good news for the reliability of the surveys.

To further examine religious practice, we asked the respondents how often they and their family members prayed (top of table 3A).

Table 3. Religious Practice and Ethnic Religious Identity by Selected Individual Characteristics (OLS Coefficients)

	A. Pray Often	B. Prayer as Ethnic Tradition
Uyghur	*0.644*	*0.503*
Hui	*0.534*	*0.642*
Kazak	*0.355*	*0.638*
Tibetan	*0.208*	
Mongol	*0.194*	*0.413*
Ethnic Other	*0.359*	*0.203*
(Han as Comparison)		
School Year	*-0.040*	-0.008
Family Income	0.037	0.001
Chinese-Language Exposure	*-0.124*	*0.168*
Communist Youth League	-0.017	*0.058*
Mixed Parents	*-0.147*	*0.065*
Female	0.016	0.002
_cons	0.279	-0.095
Adj r2	0.447	0.505
N	1469	1147

Source: 2006–2007 Chinese Ethnicity Surveys

Notes: $p <= .001$ if *italic/bold/underline*. "Pray often" is based on the question, How often do people in your family pray: never (coded 0), a few times a year (.25), monthly (.5), weekly (.75) and daily (1). "Pray for ethnic tradition" is based on the question, How much do you agree that prayer is part of your ethnic tradition? The answers include: strongly agree (1), agree (.8), somewhat agree (.6), somewhat disagree (.4), disagree (.2), and strongly disagree (0). The OLS coefficients can be interpreted as percentages. For example, in comparison with Han students, Uyghurs devoted 64.4 percent more time to prayer and were 50.3 percent more likely to see religious practice as a part of Uyghur ethnic tradition. Unfortunately, prayer as ethnic tradition was not asked in Tibet. See appendix 1 for further details.

Compared to the Hans, Muslims spent a lot more time praying: 64 percent more for the Uyghurs, 53 percent more among the Huis, and 35 percent more among the Kazaks. The Buddhists also prayed more than the Hans: 21 percent more for the Tibetans and 19 percent more for the Mongols. In other words, Muslims were the most religious group, while Buddhists were less religious than the Muslims, but more so than the "soulless" Hans.

Another question in the surveys asked the respondents whether their religious practice was related to their ethnic identity: Do you agree that praying is a part of your ethnic tradition? The answer was a uniform "yes" among minority students (top of table 3B). Compared to Han students, the Uyghurs, the Huis, the Kazaks, and even the less religious Mongol Buddhists were respectively 50 percent, 64 percent, 64 percent, and 41 percent more likely to seek ethnic identity through religious practice.

When ethnic background was controlled for, other individual characteristics also contributed to the change in prayer time. For example, in the bottom half of table 3A, each additional year in school reduced the time spent praying by 4 percent. In other words, six years of high-school education would reduce one's prayer time by about 24 percent. Chinese-language exposure also reduced the amount of time spent praying. The maximum level of Chinese-language exposure decreased prayer time by about 12 percent, regardless of one's ethnic background. Having mixed parents further discouraged prayer time by about 15 percent.

Interestingly, while Chinese-language exposure reduced the amount of time spent praying, it increased one's ethnic religious identity by about 17 percent. Similarly, while having mixed parents reduced prayer time, it promoted ethnic religious identity by about 6 percent. Finally, membership in the Communist Youth League also increased one's ethnic religious identity by 6 percent (bottom half of table 3B).

In sum, religious belief and practice were widespread among China's minorities even under the official ban, and the level of religiosity was much higher among minorities than among the Hans. Further, religious practice not only served religious purposes, it was also important in formulating ethnic identity. Finally, among other things, the findings in this section seem to suggest that the level of education, Chinese-language exposure, and political mobilization may have reduced the amount of religious practice, but they did not necessarily reduce ethnic identity, as measured by religious rituals. In fact, sinicization and political mobilization, as measured by Chinese-language exposure and Communist Youth League membership, seemed to promote ethnic identity and diversity.

Interethnic Marriage and Identity

Interethnic marriage is a measure of ethnic integration. A low level of interethnic marriage may be an indication of high ethnic awareness and social fragmentation based on ethnicity.

Earlier studies have found wide acceptance of interethnic marriage in China. For example, one study of more than 3,000 registered marriages from 1994 to 1995 in Hohhot, the capital city of Inner Mongolia, found that as many as 23 percent of Hans, 78 percent of Mongols, 99 percent of Manchus, and 33 percent of Huis married interethnically, and that there was no evidence of status consideration (marrying up) among these interethnic couples. The author attributed this ethnic integration to the socialist policy of equality and affirmative action

Earlier studies have found wide acceptance of interethnic marriage in China, which has been attributed to the socialist policy of equality and affirmative action.

(Wang 1999). Similarly, Li (2004) found a high degree of ethnic integration. By using the 2000 population census data for all interethnic couples, Li found that 42 percent of Manchus and 37 percent of Mongols intermarried with Hans, while 34 percent of Uzbeks intermarried with Uyghurs, an integration rate that the author attributed to affirmative action policies (2004, 20).

Other studies have produced similar results. Ma and Pan (1988) found a high degree of interethnic marriage between Mongols and Hans in Chifeng, Inner Mongolia. Hao's study of four villages in eastern Inner Mongolia found a sharp increase of Han-Mongol intermarriages since the 1980s (2008). Surna and Sarge (2005) showed that Mongol migrant workers in Corbog village near Hohhot had a high rate of interethnic marriage, and 84 percent of the Mongol migrant families in the study were comprised of interethnic couples with the

Hans. Xie (2006) argued that Han and Tibetan cultures shared many characteristics in common, and that the two groups had a long history of intermarriage. Xu's study of Han-Tibetan intermarriage in Labuleng Township, Gansu Province, (Xu 2005) found that Han-Tibetan intermarriages were increasingly accepted, and that the number of Han-Tibetan intermarriages nearly tripled from 1978 to 2000 (Xu 2005, 192).

Although most studies painted a positive picture of ethnic integration through marriage, they failed to explain why the overall interethnic marriage rate was only 3.2 percent of all marriages recorded in the 2000 population census (Li 2004). This low percentage shows that interethnic marriage is still a far from widely accepted practice in China. Also, some researchers were less optimistic and pointed to the difficulties in interethnic marriage. For example, Yang (2005) and Wang (2006) presented historical studies of Hui marriage, which showed that within-group marriage

> *Although most studies painted a positive picture of ethnic integration through marriage, they failed to explain why the overall interethnic marriage rate was only 3.2 percent.*

was an important way to maintain Hui identity and that the Huis were an exclusive group who would only marry other Muslims. Fang (2007) found that although Uyghurs and Kazaks were both Muslim, their linguistic and geographic distinctions prevented them from intermarrying (see also Rudelson and Jankowiak 2004). These studies, while illuminating, require further verification with empirical evidence.

In the 2006–2007 Ethnicity Surveys, we asked the respondents whether interethnic marriage was acceptable: In your opinion, is it acceptable to marry someone from the following groups? The choices included Han, foreigner, Uyghur, Hui, and Kazak. For each and every group, the respondents were asked to pick one answer, from very unacceptable (coded 0), somewhat unacceptable (.33), somewhat acceptable (.66), to very acceptable (1). The marriage preferences of the five groups—Han, foreigner, Uyghur, Hui, and Kazak—were examined in OLS (ordinary least squares) regressions against the students' individual characteristics, including ethnic background, school year, gender, family income, Chinese-language exposure, membership in the Communist Youth League, and ethnic mixture of parents. These individual-level factors can test the impact of several theoretically relevant variables discussed in earlier studies (see above), such as religion (ethnicity), modernization (school year), tradition (gender), socioeconomic status (family income), sinicization (Chinese-language exposure), political mobilization (Communist Youth League membership), and cultural fusion (mixed parents).

Ethnicity played a clear negative role in interethnic marriage rates (top of table 4). All ethnic groups expressed disapproval of marrying someone from outside their own group. Without exception, this negative feeling was quite strong and statistically significant. This finding suggests that ethnic distinction is by far the norm, rather than ethnic integration.

Further comparisons between the groups reveal some interesting differences. Han students were more likely to approve marrying a foreigner than any of the minority groups. Their disapproval of marrying Kazaks was stronger than marrying Uyghurs or Huis. As expected, Hui students disapproved marrying anyone but other Huis. Somewhat unexpectedly, Hui students did not seem to show a Muslim preference, as suggested by some studies (Wang 2006; Yang 2005). Although they reported the least disapproval to marriage with Uyghur Muslims, the Huis rated both Kazak Muslims and foreigners as least preferable of all. Mongol students expressed more tolerance of the Hans and, to a lesser extent, the Uyghurs, but disliked the Kazaks, Huis, and foreigners. Interestingly, Tibetan students seemed to tolerate Uyghurs more than other groups. Similar to the Huis, Mongols showed the least acceptance of Kazaks and foreigners. Compared with Han, Hui, Mongol, and Tibetan students, Uyghurs were the most exclusive and expressed the strongest negative feelings about marrying into other groups. They were the most

> *All ethnic groups expressed strong disapproval of marrying someone from outside their group, which suggests that ethnic distinction is by far the norm, rather than ethnic integration.*

Table 4. Interethnic Marriage by Selected Individual
Characteristics (OLS Coefficients)

	Han	Foreigner	Uyghur	Hui	Kazak
Is It Acceptable to Marry:					
Han			*-0.080*	*-0.096*	*-0.232*
Hui	*-0.147*	*-0.216*	*-0.067*		*-0.232*
Mongol	*-0.088*	*-0.192*	*-0.172*	*-0.254*	*-0.385*
Tibetan	*-0.173*	*-0.258*	*-0.040*	*-0.133*	*-0.218*
Uyghur	*-0.268*	*-0.511*		*-0.186*	*-0.300*
Kazak	*-0.294*	*-0.466*	*-0.121*	*-0.185*	
Ethnic Other	*-0.154*	*-0.256*	*-0.061*	*-0.135*	*-0.227*
School Year	*0.007*	*0.044*	0.002	-0.001	0.004
Family Income	*-0.046*	-0.018	0.001	-0.008	0.003
Chinese-Language Exposure	*0.073*	*0.101*	-0.008	*0.056*	*0.041*
Communist Youth League	*0.014*	*0.066*	0.006	*0.022*	*0.024*
Mixed Parents	-0.018	*0.063*	*0.032*	*0.027*	*0.049*
Female	-0.002	-0.023	-0.003	0.000	-0.007
_cons	*0.888*	*0.575*	*0.946*	*0.900*	*0.904*
adj r2	0.500	0.315	*0.309*	*0.239*	*0.239*
N	1510	1510	*1510*	*1510*	*1510*

Source: 2006–2007 Chinese Ethnicity Surveys

Notes: p<=.05 if italic/bold, p<=.001 if ***italic/bold/underline***. A blank cell indicates that that ethnic group is being used as a comparison group and all other coefficients in the same column should compare with the blank group. For each dependent variable, imputation is performed in Stata 10 to estimate a small number of missing values based on the respondents' answers to other relevant questions. See appendix 1 for further details of the variables.

xenophobic about foreigners and, to a lesser degree, about Kazaks and Hans. Although still quite negative, the Uyghurs reported some tolerance for the Huis. Finally, the Kazaks were quite strongly opposed to marrying foreigners and Hans, but less so to marrying Uyghurs and Huis.

These findings indicate that the Han students, as the majority in Chinese society, were the least exclusive in their marriage preferences, followed by the historically more integrated Huis and Mongols and the culturally more similar Tibetans (Xie 2006). The most exclusive were the Uyghurs and Kazaks, but there was no harmony even between these two groups. Second, the fact that the Hans were not singled out as the least-preferred group even by the most exclusive Uyghurs and Kazaks is also worth noting. The Hans were disliked not because of the specific culture they represent, but, perhaps, because they were seen as "foreigners." This is supported by the fact that marrying a foreigner was just as unacceptable, and often the most unacceptable option, for all the minority groups. Finally, while religious orientation was useful in predicting marriage choices, it was not always reliable, as the Kazaks were not necessarily accepted by their Hui and Uyghur counterparts. Other factors, such as linguistic and geographic differences, may be more important than religion (Fang 2007).

In addition to ethnic background, other socioeconomic characteristics also affected interethnic marriage decisions (bottom of table 4). Public-school education (School Year) increased one's likelihood of preferring marriage to both the Hans and foreigners, suggesting a favorable impact of modernization in ethnic integration (measured by year of education). Students from the lowest family-income group showed a 5 percent greater preference for marrying a Han. Perhaps this is an indication that marrying a Han would improve one's eco-

> *Chinese-language exposure increased the probability of marrying a Han, but it also increased the possibility of marrying a foreigner, a Hui, or a Kazak.*

nomic status, resulting in "marrying up." Contrary to the findings in an earlier study (Wang 1999), socialist affirmative action policy did not seem to entirely eliminate the economic gap between the Han majority and ethnic minorities, though the difference was small. Chinese-language exposure increased the probability of marrying a Han, but it also increased the possibility of marrying a foreigner, a Hui, or even a Kazak. Measured by Chinese-language exposure, sinicization, therefore, did not seem to mean that one could only accept the Han people. Membership in the Communist Youth League played a similarly positive role by promoting interethnic marriage. Political mobilization did not simply promote the acceptance of Han culture, but, instead, seemed to encourage the acceptance of all cultures. Understandably, having ethnically mixed parents led to greater approval of marrying someone with a minority background. In other words, the existing level of ethnic integration would provide a favorable basis for further integration. Finally, without controlling for other factors, previous studies showed a significant difference among women, who were found to be more exclusive (Wang 2006). However, when variables such as ethnic background, education, income, Chinese-language level, political mobilization, and social integration were taken into consideration, being a woman did not make any difference in marriage decisions.

We would like to reiterate several points in order to conclude this section. First, the overall level of ethnic integration is very low, and the mutual exclusion among ethnic groups is very high. Unlike some of the earlier studies that depicted China as an ethnically integrated society, the findings in this section suggest that it is a highly disintegrated society when it comes to interethnic marriage. Second, the most exclusive groups are the Uyghurs and the Kazaks, perhaps due to their lack of historical interaction with other groups and their linguistic differences and geographic locations. Third, the officially designed assimilation policies, such as improvement of socioeconomic status, Chinese-language learning, and political recruitment into the Communist Youth League, did lead to greater acceptance of the Han people among minorities. This is not surprising. Somewhat unexpected is the

> *Unlike earlier studies that depicted China as an ethnically integrated society, the findings suggest that it is a highly disintegrated society when it comes to interethnic marriage.*

unintended consequences of these assimilation policies, as they also led to greater ethnic tolerance of all groups, not only the Han people. In other words, assimilation does not mean one has to become Han.

National and Ethnic Identities: China, the United States, and Russia

So far we have compared ethnic identities in China and found strong feelings of ethnic identity by examining ethnic-language identity, religious identity, and interethnic marriage. In this section, we will examine national identity among various ethnic groups. Earlier studies have shown that nationalism has been growing among the Han population since the 1990s (Song et al. 1996; Xu 2001; Gries 2004a and 2004b). One would expect a higher level of national identity among Hans than among minorities, or, at the very least, the Hans should have an equally high level of ethnic

> *The findings about language, religion, and marriage indicate a high level of ethnic identity among minorities, but not whether they also identified themselves as belonging to a Chinese nation-state.*

identity if nationalism is understood as rooted in Han culture. The findings about language, religion, and marriage in previous sections indicate a high level of ethnic identity among minorities. It is not clear, however, whether the minority groups identified themselves as belonging to a Chinese nation-state.

We used direct measures of ethnic and national identities rather than indirect measures such as language, religion, and marriage. The 2006–2007 Chinese Ethnicity Survey asked two relevant questions. The first was a direct measure of national identity: "How close do you feel to your country?" The second question was a direct measure of ethnic identity: "How close do you feel to your ethnic group?" The respondents could choose from "not close at all" (coded 0), "not very close" (coded .333), "close" (coded .666), and "very close" (coded 1).

Table 5 shows the results of national and ethnic identities in China. Since the feeling scale ranged from 0 to 1 (see above for coding method), the average feeling for each group is a value between 0 and 1. We

Table 5. National and Ethnic Identity in China
(Feeling Thermometer 0–100)

Ethnicity	Country ID	Ethnic ID
Han	89	80
Hui	90	89
Mongol	90	91
Tibetan	89	91
Kazak	89	95
Uyghur	90	96

Source: 2006–2007 Chinese Ethnicity Surveys
Note: Data represent high school students from seventh to twelfth grades. Country ID =
"How close do you feel to your country?" Ethnic ID = "How close do you feel to
your ethnic group?" See appendix 1 for the number of cases in each ethnic group
in China.

multiplied this value by 100. The result can be interpreted as an average feeling thermometer ranging from 0 to 100.

The level of national identity in China in 2006 and 2007 was ex-
tremely high among the Hans, as well as among minorities (90 out
of 100), and there was virtually no difference among the minority
groups.[16] It is understandable that the Hans were highly nationalistic,
but it is surprising that minority students also showed a high level of
national identity. It is certainly possible that this was a result of the
official policy of mobilizing Chinese nationalism that began with the
post-Mao reforms in the late 1970s. The question is whether this nationalism was based on the dominant Han Chinese culture, or if it
represented a broader sense of Chineseness that included all the groups
equally. The finding of uniformly high national identity suggests that
Chinese nationalism may not be Han-dominated, but may include all
groups equally, at least in principle.

The results of ethnic identity in China are interesting. Minority
students reported equally high degrees (around 90) of ethnic identity
and national identity. If this was a result of political mobilization and
propaganda, it further pointed to the inclusiveness of such propaganda, rather than the promoting of Han domination. This is not to say
that minorities were treated equally in reality. But the slogan of ethnic
equality did seem to promote ethnic awareness, which, in turn, could

be used to mobilize political resistance. The Han ethnic-identity score was also quite high (80), but it was 9–16 percent less than that reported by minority students.

One way to verify the uniqueness of the high level of national identity among China's minorities is to compare China with other societies. We will compare China with the United States and Russia. These three countries share an important demographic characteristic, in that all have a dominant majority. In the United States, almost 82 percent of the population in 2003 was classified as white. In Russia, almost 80 percent of the population in 2002 was ethnic Russian. In China, almost 92 percent of the population was Han.[17] Despite their demographic similarities, the three countries operate in entirely different political environments. The United States is an established democracy, Russia is a new democracy, and China is authoritarian. It is possible that these different political systems will generate different patterns of national identity.

In the United States, studies have found that minorities, particularly African Americans, showed a lower level of national identity than the white majority (Huddy and Khatib 2007). These findings would lead one to expect a higher level of national identity among whites than non-whites. It is unclear whether ethnic identity would be high among minorities. On the one hand, African Americans, who are by far the largest minority group (13 percent of the total population), were stripped of their African cultural ties during the slave trade. Few public schools use a non-English language as the teaching language. Minorities seem to be more assimilated and should, therefore, have relatively strong feelings of national identity. Further, the terrorist attack on the World Trade Center in 2001 may have aroused feelings of nationalism in the United States. What is not immediately clear is whether the September 11 attack affected the white majority and minority groups in the same way or differently.

In Russia, regional diversity and the lack of a common understanding and consensus about history (Peterson 2001; Hesli 2007) have led

> *In the United States, studies have found that minorities showed a lower level of national identity than the white majority.*

to a weak feeling of national identity among both the Russian majority and the non-Russian minorities. Further, national identity is likely
to be weakened due to the country's more than 70 years' history of
communism. The socialist ethnic policy was based on state-sponsored
affirmative action, which strengthened ethnic-group awareness. Ethnic
awareness then gained further political ground during the breakup of
the Soviet Union (Karklins 1987; Martin 2001). In the post–Soviet
Russian Federation, ethnic minorities were able to negotiate additional
autonomy with Moscow, and the increased ethnic autonomy posed
further challenges to building a new multinational state among the
Russian majority and ethnic minorities (Hesli 2007). As a result, one
would expect a relatively weak feeling of nationalism in Russia.

To measure national identity in the United States and Russia, we
used three questions from the 2003 National Identity Surveys (II),
conducted by the International Social Survey Programme (ISSP):[18]

1) I would rather be a citizen of [COUNTRY] than of any other country in the world.
2) Generally speaking, [COUNTRY] is a better country than most
   other countries.
3) When my country does well in international sports, it makes me
   proud to be [COUNTRY NATIONALITY].

For each question, the respondents were asked to pick one of the
following answers: disagree strongly (coded 0), disagree (coded 1), neither agree nor disagree (coded 2), agree (coded 3), and agree strongly (coded 4). High values indicate more national identity than low values. The three questions were com-
bined into an additive index, which was then converted into a national identity index, with a scale ranging from 0 (no identity) to 100 (maximum identity).[19]

The 2008 China Survey was used to make the data from the three countries more comparable.

Since the 2006–2007 Chinese Ethnicity Surveys only surveyed
high-school students, it is not ideal to compare it with the ISSP survey
in the United States and Russia, which covers the entire adult population

in these countries. In order to make the data from the three countries more comparable, we used the 2008 China Survey, which is a project of the College of Liberal Arts at Texas A&M University, in collaboration with the Research Center for Contemporary China (RCCC) at Peking University.[20] This survey is based on a national random sample of 3,989 adult respondents in 146 townships, 73 counties, and 25 provinces. The spatial sampling technique ensures a realistic representation of the migrant population, which is difficult to catch with traditional methods of household registration. More importantly, the 2008 China Survey contains the same three questions on national identity as the 2003 ISSP National Identity Survey in the United States and Russia, making it possible to compare China with these countries.

One problem with the 2008 China Survey is the small number of minority respondents.[21] However, the sample does include adequate numbers among two important ethnic groups, Hui and Uyghur. There are 58 Huis and 83 Uyghurs, in addition to 3,408 Han respondents. Consequently, in China, we will only be able to compare national identities among these three groups. In the United States, European Americans (white) will be compared with African, Latino, and Asian Americans. In Russia, Russians will be compared with the mostly Muslim Tatars and Armenians.

In the 2008 China Survey, the Han majority demonstrated a slightly lower level of national identity than the Huis and Uyghurs.

Figure 2 shows the average scores of national identity among different ethnic groups in China, the United States, and Russia. In the 2008 China Survey, both Huis and Uyghurs continued to show very high levels of national identity (89 and 87). These findings confirm the similar results shown in table 5. The Han majority, on the other hand, demonstrated a slightly lower level of national identity (84) than the Huis and Uyghurs.

One potential problem of the strong national identity among the two minority groups is the possibility that these respondents were under political pressure and fear of reprisal if they revealed their true resentment against the Chinese nation-state. One way to check the

Figure 2. Nationalism by Ethnicity in China, the United States, and Russia, Weighted (Max=100)

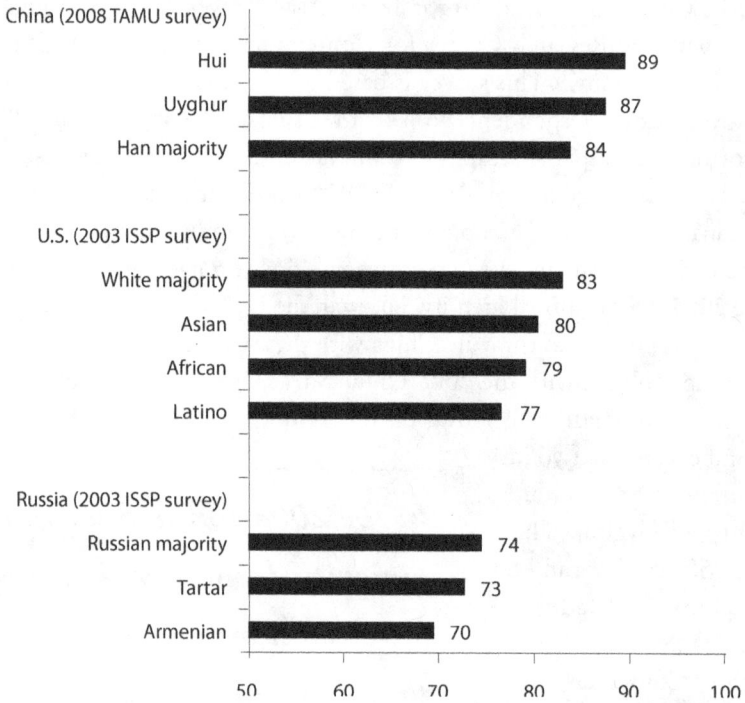

Source: 2008 Texas A&M China Survey and 2003 International Social Survey Programme National Identity Surveys (II).
Note: The nationalism index (0-100) is based on three questions in the surveys: 1) I would rather be a citizen of [COUNTRY] than of any other country in the world; 2) Generally speaking, [COUNTRY] is a better country than most other countries; 3) When my country does well in international sports, it makes me proud to be [COUNTRY NATIONALITY]. For the United States, the number of cases for each group is: White=941, Asian=33, African=154, Latino=32. For Russia, Russian=1,803, Armenian=52, Tartar=82. For China, Han=2,942, Hui=45, Uyghur=77 (missing values are excluded).

reliability of the minorities' strong national identity is to see how they answered other politically sensitive questions. One such question in the 2008 China Survey was, "Everyone should support the government even if it is in the wrong." The minorities should give the same affirmative answer to this question as they gave to the question about national identity if political fear was a factor. The results show that on a 0–100 scale, the Han respondents scored 46 in their approval of this question, while the Huis and the Uyghurs only scored 34 and 37 respectively.[22] These low scores suggest that the respondents in general, and the minority respondents in particular, of the 2008 China Survey were not especially afraid to express their true feelings on politically sensitive questions. They also give us more confidence in accepting the findings of high levels of national identity among China's minority groups.

In the United States, the European American majority showed a comparable level of national identity (83) to the Hans in China. White Americans' national identity was slightly higher than that of Asian Americans, African Americans, and Latino Americans, but these differences were not statistically significant. Further examination, however, of only the third question relating to whether the respondent was proud to be a citizen of the United States indicated that Latinos had a lower level (79) of pride than white Americans (91), a gap that was statistically sig-

If national identity is measured by whether the respondent was proud to be a citizen of his/her country, the findings confirm a weak national identity among U.S. minorities, particularly Latinos.

nificant. Therefore, if national identity is measured by only one of the three questions in the 2003 ISSP National Identity Survey, i.e., proud to be a citizen, the findings in this study confirm the earlier study that found a weak national identity among minorities in the United States (Huddy and Khatib 2007), particularly among Latinos.

In Russia, the Russian majority showed slightly higher levels of national identity than Tatars and Armenians, both of whom are Muslim minorities, but the difference was not statistically significant. When we only used the question on being proud to be a Russian citizen, however, Armenians reported less enthusiasm (67) than both Russians (77) and Tatars (78), and this lack of Russian identity among Armenians was statistically significant at $p < .05$. Unfortunately, in the Russian sample of the 2003 ISSP National Identity Survey, Tatars and Armenians were the only minority groups with sufficient numbers of respondents for statistical analysis. It is possible that other ethnic minorities, such as those in the North Caucasus, would report significantly weaker levels of national identity than the Russian majority if there had been enough survey respondents from these groups to analyze.[23]

Overall, the Russian respondents in the 2003 ISSP National Identity Survey scored lower on national identity (74, the average of all groups) than China (84) and the United States (82). Among other reasons, this low level of national identity seems to reflect the lack of historical consensus about national identity and the breakup of the USSR. Russian residents in 2003 were still experiencing Russia's declining international status as a superpower, and the Russian economy had still not fully recovered from the breakup of the Soviet Union.[24] For example, Russia's per capita gross domestic product in 2002 was still lower than it had been before the collapse of central planning in 1990.[25] All these factors, perhaps, contributed to the lower level of national identity in Russia, while the September 11 terrorist attack in the United States and the rapid economic growth and rising international importance of China seemed to arouse stronger feelings of nationalism in both countries.

> *Overall, the Russian respondents in the 2003 ISSP National Identity Survey scored lower on national identity (74) than China (84) and the United States (82).*

In the previous sections, we found strong ethnic identity among China's religious ethnic minorities by examining ethnic-language identity, religious identity, and interethnic marriage. In this section, we used more survey questions to measure the respondents' direct feelings of ethnic and national identities. In addition to confirming the strong ethnic identity found in the previous sections, one piece of important new information found in this section is that the religious minorities in China also reported a strong identity with the Chinese nation-state, and that this identity is stronger in China than the national identity of minorities in other countries. China seems to be unique in producing equally strong ethnic and national identities (see table 1), at least when comparing it with the United States and Russia.

Conclusion: Equality and Loyalty

Ethnic policy in China is a combination of the Qing legacy and socialist affirmative action. By inheriting the ethnic policy of their Qing predecessors, the Communists did not build a country based on Han superiority, at least not in their rhetoric. Instead, they built a multieth-nic society in which all groups are equal, but must also remain loyal to the socialist state. The Qing rulers once used political marriages to appease ethnic minorities. Today's Chinese leaders are trying to achieve the same goals as the Qing emperors did by sending economic aid to minority-occupied regions and by implementing state-sponsored affir-mative action programs. These programs are not designed just to show respect for minority cultures, as stated in the Communist Party's pro-paganda; rather, they are ultimately designed to give minorities a stake in remaining a part of China. The party leaders are very aware that disruptive relations with minority groups can lead to the disintegration of the Chinese nation-state.

As we have shown in this study, the Chinese state has so far man-aged to keep ethnic tension under control by using affirmative ac-tion to promote Chinese identity among minorities. This success is not exclusively based on the use of force, although that is always held up as an option. The religious minorities seem to willingly accept being Chinese if, and only if, being Chinese means being culturally autonomous and the minority groups are allowed to keep their own languages, religions, and marriage practices. It is a negotiated contract be-tween the state and the minorities. The problem for China is not so much Han mistreatment of minorities, which is by no means absent. The more serious problem is how long this delicate

> *Religious minorities seem to accept being Chinese if that means being culturally autonomous and being allowed to keep their own languages, religions, and marriage practices.*

balancing act between nationalism and ethnic identity will last. In the 2009 Urumqi riot, the Uyghur protesters did not advocate break-ing away from China, but demanded their separate-but-equal status under the Chinese Constitution, and they demonstrated with the Chinese flag.[26] For the time being, the state has been the recipient of minority loyalty by keeping minorities separate from Han culture. If the state fails to continue to promote ethnic identity and guarantee affirmative action and some degree of autonomy, then being Chinese could lose its attraction, and the fragile balance between the state and the minorities would collapse.

In the future, ethnic tension is likely to escalate if state-sponsored affirmative action continues its current pattern of interaction with market reforms. Affirmative action has promoted a strong sense of ethnic identity, group awareness, and pride. Market reforms have increased population mobility, labor-market competition, and income inequality. In an individual-based society, people blame themselves for not finding jobs and for being poor. In an affirmative action–based society, people see their losses in market competition as a result of being a member of a minority group, and they blame the state. Ironically, affirmative action, when combined with market competition, creates more ethnic tension. The riots in Tibet in 2008 and Xinjiang in 2009 were good examples of the escalating tension that arose after the state poured massive amounts of economic aid into the regions over the past two decades.

Appendix 1. Characteristics of the 2006–2007 Ethnicity Surveys

Variable	Obs	Mean	Std. Dev.	Min	Max
Importance of language					
ethnic	1598	.3003755	.3141393	0	1
Chinese	1598	.3619107	.266559	0	1
English	1598	.2824364	.2598834	0	1
Studying language for culture					
ethnic	1598	.3197748	.2534995	0	1
Chinese	1598	.2233686	.3402127	0	1
English	1598	.1787391	.273755	0	1
pray often	1544	.3944301	.3884196	0	1
prayer culture	1219	.4004649	.3511011	0	1
Inter-ethnic marriage:					
wedhan	1598	.7707934	.172829	0	1
weduyghur	1598	.9086698	.0943123	0	1
wedhui	1598	.8171073	.1192731	0	1
wedkazak	1598	.7392388	.1660523	0	1
wedoth	1598	.6816244	.1560263	0	1
wedalien	1598	.4751462	.3932642	0	1
Tibetan	1598	.2371715	.4254814	0	1
Han	1598	.2302879	.4211489	0	1
Mongol	1598	.0350438	.1839481	0	1
Uyghur	1598	.3435544	.4750432	0	1
Hui	1598	.0394243	.1946631	0	1
Kazak	1598	.0813517	.27346	0	1
Ethnic Other	1598	.0331665	.1791271	0	1
school yr	1571	3.437938	1.366734	1	6
7th grade	1571	.0579249	.2336757	0	1
8th grade	1571	.298536	.4577615	0	1

Wenfang Tang and Gaochao He

Appendix 1 (continued). Characteristics of the 2006–2007 Ethnicity Surveys

Variable	Obs	Mean	Std. Dev.	Min	Max
9th grade	1571	.0706556	.2563303	0	1
10th grade	1571	.3520051	.4777476	0	1
11th grade	1571	.162317	.3688588	0	1
12th grade	1571	.0585614	.2348768	0	1
female	1598	.5225282	.4996486	0	1
family inc	1563	.4937945	.2283657	0	1
Chn-lng exposure	1563	.6470282	.3043697	0	1
Comm Youth League	1598	.635169	.4815334	0	1

Appendix 2. Schools and classes in the 2006–2007 Chinese Ethnicity Surveys (school names are kept anonymous to protect the respondents)

	Freq.	Percent	Cum.
School 1, class 1	38	2.38	2.38
School 2, class 2	51	3.19	5.57
School 3, class 3	55	3.44	9.01
School 4, class 4	60	3.75	12.77
School 4, class 5	50	3.13	15.89
School 5, class 6	58	3.63	19.52
School 5, class 7	30	1.88	21.40
School 6, class 8	50	3.13	24.53
School 7, class 9	41	2.57	27.10
School 7, class 10	44	2.75	29.85
School 8, class 11	52	3.25	33.10
School 8, class 12	49	3.07	36.17
School 9, class 13	49	3.07	39.24
School 9, class 14	35	2.19	41.43
School 10, class 15	43	2.69	44.12
School 10, class 16	43	2.69	46.81
School 10, class 17	44	2.75	49.56
School 11, class 18	42	2.63	52.19
School 11, class 19	23	1.44	53.63
School 11, class 20	34	2.13	55.76
School 12, class 21	80	5.01	60.76
School 12, class 22	28	1.75	62.52
School 13, class 23	51	3.19	65.71
School 13, class 24	55	3.44	69.15
School 14, class 25	52	3.25	72.40
School 14, class 26	54	3.38	75.78
School 14, class 27	46	2.88	78.66
School 14, class 28	46	2.88	81.54
School 15, class 29	45	2.82	84.36

Wenfang Tang and Gaochao He

Appendix 2 (continued). Schools and classes in the 2006–2007 Chinese Ethnicity Surveys (school names are kept anonymous to protect the respondents)

	Freq.	Percent	Cum.
School 16, class 30	48	3.00	87.36
School 17, class 31	50	3.13	90.49
School 17, class 32	54	3.38	93.87
School 17, class 33	63	3.94	97.81
School 17, class 34	33	2.07	99.87
Unidentified	2	0.13	100.00
Total	1,598		100.00

Endnotes

1. For the sometimes arbitrary classification and formation of the 56 ethnic groups in 1953, see Ma 2000.

2. See http://english.people.com.cn/constitution/constitution.html, checked March 15, 2010.

3. According to Professor Wang Songtao, associate dean of the School of Foreign Languages at Inner Mongolia University, about 30–40 percent of the freshman class each year at his university was Mongol. This was much higher than the 18 percent Mongolian population in Inner Mongolia. Interview notes, Inner Mongolia University, Hohhot, China, May 24, 2008.

4. One anonymous reviewer suggested that part of the minority population growth is the result of affirmative action policies. People with mixed Han-ethnic backgrounds were motivated to report themselves as members of minority groups in order to enjoy affirmative action benefits, such as getting admitted into universities and finding jobs.

5. For examples of the overseas Uyghur separatist organizations, see the German-based Eastern Turkistan Information Center (http://www.uygur.org/english) and the U.S.-based World Uyghur Congress (http://www.uyghurcongress.org/en/), checked March 15, 2010.

6. See http://www.chinadaily.com.cn/china/2009-07/11/content_8415245.htm, checked March 15, 2010.

7. Great Britain also played an important role in the relationship between Tibet and China in the first half of the twentieth century. In 1904, it invaded Tibet and promised Tibetan independence if Tibet paid the indemnity for the invasion. In 1906, the Qing government paid the bill in return for Great Britain's consent that China have sovereignty over Tibet, though China agreed to Tibetan autonomy. The Nationalist government followed the 1906 Sino-British Peking Convention from 1911 to 1951.

8. See http://www.tibet.com/, checked March 15, 2010.

9. There is a large amount of literature on Tibet. For the history of Tibet, see Goldstein 1989, 1997, and 2004; Grunfeld 1996; Shakya 1999; Feigon 2000; Heath 2005. For the U.S. involvement in Tibet, see Dunham 2004; Laird 2002; Grunfeld 2006; Goldstein 1991, 1999, and 2004. For social and economic development in Tibet, see Goldstein et al. 2006; Dreyer 2006; Norbu 2006; and Sautman 2006. For village life in rural Tibet, see Yu 2006.

10. This is in China only. The population in the Republic of Mongolia is about 3 million (https://www.cia.gov/library/publications/the-world-factbook/print/mg.html).

11. See http://www.innermongolia.org/english/index.html, checked June 28, 2008.

12. See http://www.issp.org/data.shtml, checked June 27, 2008.

13. See http://news.xinhuanet.com/edu/2002-01/21/content_246175.htm, checked July 1, 2008.

14. Professor Teng Xing at the China Central Nationalities University in Beijing made this point during a conversation on January 8, 2008.

15. See http://www.seac.gov.cn/gjmw/zcfg/2004-07-10/1168742761853498.htm, checked July 1, 2008.

16. We further compared national identity among the six grades and did not find any significant difference.

17. See the *2008 CIA World Factbook* (https://www.cia.gov/library/publications/the-world-factbook/index.html, checked July 4, 2008).

18. See http://www.gesis.org/en/data_service/issp/data/2003_National_Identity_II.htm, checked July 4, 2008.

19. Since each question ranges from 0 to 4, the index is constructed by adding the three questions, dividing the result by 12, and then multiplying it by 100.

20. We would like to express our appreciation to Professor Robert Harmel at Texas A&M University for generously sharing this dataset.

21. For example, there are only 8 Mongolians, 1 Tibetan, and no Kazaks.

22. The differences between the Hans and the Huis and Uyghurs were statistically significant at $p<=.05$ and $p<=.10$.

23. In the Russian sample, only Tatars and Armenians had adequate numbers of cases (82 and 52), in addition to Russians (1,803). There were only 24 Ukrainians, 12 Belarusians, 11 Jews, and less than 5 respondents in each of the remaining groups (Chinese, Finnish, German, Greek, Italian, Kurdish, Latvian, and Polish).

24. We wish to thank Vicki Hesli for reminding us of plausible explanations for Russia's low national identity in the 2003 ISSP survey.

25. Per capita GDP based on purchasing power parity in Russia was $8,230 in 2002 and $8,340 in 1990. See http://globalis.gvu.unu.edu/indicator_detail.cfm?IndicatorID=19&Country=RU, checked 3/20/10.

26. This flag flying was reported by several sources, including http://chinaworker.info/zh/content/news/787/, *Los Angeles Times* (July 6, 2009), and www.uyghuramerican.org//articles/3103/.

Bibliography

Anderson, Benedict. 1991. *Imagined Communities: Reflections on the Origin and Spread of Nationalism.* Rev. ed. London and New York: Verso.

Backman, David. 2004. "Making Xinjiang Safe for the Han? Contradictions and Ironies of Chinese Governance in China's Northwest." In Morris Rossabi, ed. *Governing China's Multiethnic Frontiers,* Seattle and London: University of Washington Press.

Barnet, Robert. 2006. "Beyond the Collaborator-Martyr Model: Strategies of Compliance, Opportunism, and Opposition within Tibet." In Barry Sautman and June Teufel Dreyer, eds. *Contemporary Tibet: Politics, Development, and Society in a Disputed Region.* New York: M.E. Sharpe.

Barrington, Lowell W. 2002. "Examining Rival Theories of Demographic Influences on Political Support: The Power of Regional, Ethnic, and Linguistic Divisions in Ukraine." *European Journal of Political Research* 41: 455–91.

Bass, Catriona. 2005. "Learning to Love the Motherland: Educating Tibetans in China." *Journal of Moral Education* 34(4): 433–49.

Benson, Linda. 2004. "Education and Social Mobility among Minority Populations in Xinjiang." In S. Frederick Starr, ed. *Xinjiang: China's Muslim Borderland.* New York: M.E. Sharpe.

Bovingdon, Gardner. 2004a. "Autonomy in Xinjiang: Han Nationalist Imperatives and Uyghur Discontent." *Policy Studies* 11. Washington, DC: East-West Center.

———. 2004b. "Heteronomy and Its Discontents: 'Minzu Regional Autonomy' in Xinjiang." In Morris Rossabi, ed. *Governing China's Multiethnic Frontiers.* Seattle and London: University of Washington Press.

———, with contributions by Nabijan Tursun. 2004c. "Contested Histories." In S. Frederick Starr, ed. *Xinjiang: China's Muslim Borderland.* New York: M.E. Sharpe.

Bulag, Uradyn E. 2004. "Inner Mongolia: The Dialectics of Colonization and Ethnicity Building." In Morris Rossabi, ed. *Governing China's Multiethnic Frontiers.* Seattle and London: University of Washington Press.

Burjgin, Jirgal and Naran Bilik. 2003. "Contemporary Mongolian Population Distribution, Migration, Cultural Change, and Identity." In Robyn Iredale, Naran Bilik, and Fei Guo, eds. *China's Minorities on the Move: Selected Case Studies*. New York: M.E. Sharpe.

Chia, Ning. 1993. "The Lifanyuan and the Inner Asian Rituals in the Early Qing (1644–1795)." *Late Imperial China* 14(1): 60–92.

Clothey, Rebecca. 2005. "China's Policies for Ethnic Minority Studies: Negotiating National Values and Ethnic Identities." *Comparative Education Review* 49(3): 389–409.

Crossley, Pamela K. 1985. "An Introduction to the Qing Foundation Myth." *Late Imperial China* 6(2): 13–36.

Dikötter, Frank. 1992. *The Discourse of Race in Modern China*. Stanford: Stanford University Press.

Dow, Tsung-I. 1982. "The Confucian Concept of a Nation and Its Historical Practice." *Asian Profile* 10(4): 347–61.

Dreyer, June Teufel. 2006. "Economic Development in Tibet Under the People's Republic of China." In Barry Sautman and June Teufel Dreyer, eds. *Contemporary Tibet: Politics, Development, and Society in a Disputed Region*. New York: M.E. Sharpe.

Dunham, Mikel. 2004. *Buddha's Warriors: The Story of the CIA-Backed Tibetan Freedom Fighters, the Chinese Invasion, and the Ultimate Fall of Tibet*. New York: Jeremy P. Tarcher/Penguin.

Dwyer, Arienne M. 2005. "The Xinjiang Conflict: Uyghur Identity, Language Policy, and Political Discourse." *Policy Studies* 15. Washington, DC: East-West Center.

East Turkistan Information Center [东土耳其斯坦信息中心]. 2005. "A Brief History of the Uyghurs." http://www.uygur.org/enorg/history/history.htm, checked August 16, 2005.

Fang, Ruoyu [房若愚]. 2007. "新疆族际通婚圈的文化成因" [The Cause Analyses of Ethnic Intermarriage in Xinjiang]. 西北人口 [*Northwest Population*] 28(3): 84–8.

Feigon, Lee. 1999. *Demystifying Tibet: Unlocking the Secrets of the Land of the Snows*. London: Profile Books.

Fuller, Graham E., and Jonathan N. Lipman. 2004. "Islam in Xinjiang." In S. Frederick Starr, ed. *Xinjiang: China's Muslim Borderland*. New York: M.E. Sharpe.

Gao, Mei [高梅]. 2006. "语言与民族认同" [Language and Ethnic Identity]. 满族研究 [*Manchu Studies*], 4: 47–51.

Gladney, Dru C. 1991. *Muslim Chinese: Ethnic Nationalism in the People's Republic*. Cambridge: Harvard University Press.

———. 1996. "Relational Alterity: Constructing Dungan (Hui), Uygur, and Kazahk Identities across China, Central Asia, and Turkey." *History and Anthropology* 9(2): 1–33.

———. 1998. *Ethnic Identity in China: The Making of A Muslim Minority Nationality.* Fort Worth: Harcourt Brace College Publishers.

———. 1998. *Ethnic Identity in China: The Making of A Muslim Minority Nationality.* Fort Worth: Harcourt Brace College Publishers.

———. 2004a. *Dislocating China: Reflections on Muslims, Minorities, and Other Subaltern Subjects.* Chicago: University of Chicago Press.

———. 2004b. "The Chinese Program of Development and Control, 1978–2001." In S. Frederick Starr, ed. *Xinjiang: China's Muslim Borderland.* New York: M.E. Sharpe.

———. 2004c. "Responses to Chinese Rule: Patterns of Cooperation and Opposition." In S. Frederick Starr, ed. *Xinjiang: China's Muslim Borderland.* New York: M.E. Sharpe.

Goldstein, Melvyn C. 1989. *A History of Modern Tibet: 1913–1951.* Berkeley: University of California Press.

———. 1997. *The Snow Lion and the Dragon: China, Tibet, and the Dalai Lama.* Berkeley: University of California Press.

———. 2004. "Tibet and China in the Twentieth Century." In Morris Rossabi, ed. *Governing China's Multiethnic Frontiers.* Seattle and London: University of Washington Press.

———, Jiao Ben, Cynthia M. Beall, and Phuntsog Tsering. 2006. "Development and Change in Rural Tibet: Problems and Adaptations." In Barry Sautman and June Teufel Dreyer, eds. *Contemporary Tibet: Politics, Development, and Society in a Disputed Region.* New York: M.E. Sharpe.

Greenberg, Ilan. 2008. "Changing the Rules of the Games," *New York Times*, March 30.

Gries, Peter Hays. 2004a. *China's New Nationalism: Pride, Politics and Diplomacy.* Berkeley: University of California Press.

———. 2004b. "Popular Nationalism and State Legitimation in China." In Peter Hays Gries and Stanley Rosen, eds. *State and Society in 21st Century China.* New York and London: RoutledgeCurzon.

Grunfeld, A. Tom. 1996. *The Making of Modern Tibet.* New York: M.E. Sharpe.

———. 2006. "Tibet and the United States." In Barry Sautman and June Teufel Dreyer, eds. *Contemporary Tibet: Politics, Development, and Society in a Disputed Region.* New York: M.E. Sharpe.

Hao, Yaming [郝亚明]. 2008. "乡村蒙古族婚姻的现况与变" [The Actuality and Changes of Mongolian Marriage in Rural Areas, – Based on the Village Study in Eastern Inner Mongolia]. 西北民族研究 [*N. W. Ethno-National Studies*] 56(1): 154–63

He, Baogang. 2006. "The Dalai Lama's Autonomy Proposal: A One-Sided Wish?" In Barry Sautman and June Teufel Dreyer, eds. *Contemporary Tibet: Politics, Development, and Society in a Disputed Region.* New York: M.E. Sharpe, 67–84.

He, Yuchou, and Wang Yingxi [何玉畴, 王迎喜]. 1989. "论清代对回族的政策" [The Qing Policy toward Hui]. 甘肃社会科学 [*Gansu Social Science*], 2: 61–5.

Heath, John. 2005. *Tibet and China in the Twenty-first Century*. London: SAQI Books.

Hesli, Vicki L. 2007. *Governments and Politics in Russia and the Post-Soviet Region*. New York: Houghton Mifflin.

Ho, Ping-Ti. 1967. "The Significance of the Ch'ing Period in Chinese History." *Journal of Asian Studies* 26(2): 189–95.

Hu, Yiyang. 2008. "Identity and Support for Political Communities Based on Language Choice Data in Tibet." MA thesis, University of Pittsburgh.

Hua, Li [华立]. 1983. "清代的满蒙联姻" [Manchurian and Mongolian Intermarriage in Qing Dynasty]. 民族研究 [*Ethno-National Studies*] 2: 45–54, 79.

Huddy, Leonie, and Nadia Khatib. 2007. "American Patriotism, National Identity, and Political Involvement." *American Journal of Political Science* 51: 63–77.

Isaacs, Halrold R. 1975. *Idols of the Tribe: Group Identity and Political Change*. Cambridge: Harvard University Press.

Jin Baosen [金宝森]. 1992. "浅谈乾隆对发展满文的贡献" [On Qianlong's Contribution to the Development of Manchurian Language]. 清史研究 [*Studies in Qing History*], 1: 78–80.

Jin, Zhongjie [金忠杰]. 2007. "阿拉伯语教学在宁夏的历史沿革及其民间特点" [History and Characteristics of Arabic Language Education in Ningxia]. 西北第二民族学院学报(哲学社会科学版) [*Journal of the Second Northwest University for Nationalities*], 3: 47–52.

Johnson, Bonnie, and Nalini Chhetri. 2000. "Exclusionary Policies and Practices in Chinese Minority Education: The Case of Tibetan Education." *Current Issues in Comparative Education* 2(2): 1–11.

Kahn, Joseph. 2004. "Ethnic Clashes Erupt in China, Leaving 150 Dead," *New York Times*, October 31.

Kapstein, Matthew T. 2006. "A Thorn in the Dragon's Side: Tibetan Buddhist Culture in China." In Morris Rossabi, ed. *Governing China's Multiethnic Frontiers*. Seattle and London: University of Washington Press.

Karklins, Rasma. 1987. "Nationality Policy and Ethnic Relations in the USSR." In James R. Millar, ed. *Politics, Work, and Daily Life in the USSR: A Survey of Former Soviet Citizens*. New York: Cambridge University Press.

Kolas, Ashild. 1996. "Tibetan Nationalism: The Politics of Religion." *Journal of Peace Research* 33(1): 51—66.

Laird, Thomas. 2002. *Into Tibet: The CIA's First Atomic Spy and His Secret Expedition to Lhasa*. New York: Grove Press.

Laitin, David. 2000. "What Is a Language Community?" *American Journal of Political Science* 44(1): 142—55.

Li, Xiaoxia [李晓霞]. 2004. "试论中国族际通婚圈的构成" [On the Structure of Interethnic Marriage in China]. 广西民族研究 [*Guangxi Ethno-National Studies*] 77(3): 20–7.

Lipman, Jonathan N. 1997. *Familiar Strangers: A History of the Muslims of Northwest China*. Seattle: University of Washington Press.

———. 2004. "White Hats, Oil Cakes, and Common Blood: The Hui in the Contemporary Chinese State." In Morris Rossabi, ed. *Governing China's Multiethnic Frontiers*. Seattle and London: University of Washington Press.

Ma, Rong [马戎]. 2000. 关于"民族"定义 [On the Definition of "Nationality"]. 云南民族学院学报(哲学社会科学版) [*Journal of Yunnan University of the Nationalities*] 17(1): 5–13.

——— and Danzenglunzhu [马戎、旦增伦珠]. 2006. "拉萨市流动人口调查报告" [Temporary Migration in Lhasa City]. 西北民族研究 [*N. W. Ethno-National Studies*], 51(4): 124–71.

——— and Naigu Pan [马戎、潘乃古]. 1988. "赤峰农村牧区蒙汉通婚的研究" [Mongol-Han Intermarriage in Rural Chifeng], 北京大学学报(哲学社会科学版) [*Journal of Peking University (Philosophy and Social Sciences)*], 3: 76–87.

———, Xiaoli Wang, Junxiong Fang, and Yaping Han [马戎、王晓丽、方军雄、韩亚萍]. 2005. "新疆乌鲁木齐市流动人口的结构特征与就业状况" [Structural Characters and Employment of Temporary Migrants in Wulumuqi City, Xinjiang Uygur Autonomous Region]. 西北民族研究 [*N. W. Ethno-National Studies*] 46(3): 5–42.

Mackerras, Colin 2004a. "What Is China? Who is Chinese? Han Minority Relations, Legitimacy, and the State." In Peter Hays Gries and Stanley Rosen, eds. *State and Society in 21st-Century China: Crisis, Contention, and Legitimation*. New York and London: RoutledgeCurzon.

———. 2004b. "China's Minorities and National Integration." In Leong H. Liew and Shaoguang Wang, eds. *Nationalism, Democracy and National Integration in China*. New York and London: RoutledgeCurzon.

Manion, Melanie. 1994. "Survey Research in the Study of Contemporary China: Learning from Local Samples." *China Quarterly* 139: 741–65.

———. 2010. "A Survey of Survey Research on Chinese Politics: What Have We Learned?" In Alan Carlson, Mary Gallagher, Kenneth Lieberthal, and Melanie Manion, eds. *Contemporary Chinese Politics: New Sources, Methods, and Field Strategies*. Cambridge: Cambridge University Press.

Martin, Terry. 2001. *The Affirmative Action Empire: Nations and Nationalism in the Soviet Union, 1923–1939*. The Wilder House Series in Politics, History, and Culture. Ithaca: Cornell University Press.

Millward, James A. 1998. *Beyond the Pass: Economy, Ethnicity, and Empire in Qing Central Asia, 1759–1864*. Stanford: Stanford University Press.

———. 2004. "Violent Separatism in Xinjiang: A Critical Assessment." *Policy Studies* 6. Washington, DC: East-West Center.

———— and Peter C. Perdue. 2004a. "Political and Cultural History of the Xingjiang Region through the Late Nineteenth Century." In S. Frederick Starr, ed. *Xinjiang: China's Muslim Borderland*. New York: M.E. Sharpe.

———— and Peter C. Perdue. 2004b. "Political History and Strategies of Control, 1884—1978." In S. Frederick Starr, ed. *Xinjiang: China's Muslim Borderland*. New York: M.E. Sharpe.

Nash, M. 1996. "The Core Elements of Ethnicity." In J. Hutchinson and A.D. Smith eds. *Ethnicity*. Oxford: Oxford University Press.

Norbu, Dawa. 2006. "Economic Policy and Practice in Contemporary Tibet." In Barry Sautman and June Teufel Dreyer, eds. *Contemporary Tibet: Politics, Development, and Society in a Disputed Region*. New York: M.E. Sharpe.

Peterson, Bo. 2001. *National Self-Images and Regional Identities in Russia*. Aldershot, UK: Ashgate Publishing.

Postiglione, Gerard, Ben Jiao, and Sonam Gyatso. 2005. "Education in Rural Tibet: Development, Problems and Adaptations." *China: An International Journal* 3(1): 1–23.

Rawski, Evelyn S. 1991. "Ch'ing Imperial Marriage and Problems of Rulership." In Rubie S. Watson and Patricia B. Ebrey, eds. *Marriage and Inequality in Chinese Society*. Berkeley and Los Angeles: University of California Press.

————. 1996. "Presidential Address: Reenvisioning the Qing; The Significance of the Qing Period in Chinese History." *Journal of Asian Studies* 55,(4): 829–50.

————. 2001. *The Last Emperors: A Social History of Qing Imperial Institutions*. Berkeley: University of California Press.

Reuters. 2000. "Hijack Foiled, Lone Suspect Killed," September 27.

Rossabi, Morris. 2004. "Introduction." In Morris Rossabi, ed. *Governing China's Multiethnic Frontiers*. Seattle and London: University of Washington Press.

Rudelson, Justin, and William Jankowiak. 2004. "Acculturation and Resistance: Xinjiang Identities in Flux." In S. Frederick Starr, ed. *Xinjiang: China's Muslim Borderland*. New York: M.E. Sharpe.

Sautman, Barry. 2006. "'Demographic Annihilation' and Tibet." In Barry Sautman and June Teufel Dreyer, eds. *Contemporary Tibet: Politics, Development, and Society in a Disputed Region*. New York: M.E. Sharpe.

Schiaffini, Patricia. 2004. "The Language Divide: Identity and Literary Choices in Modern Tibet." *Journal of International Affairs* 57 (Spring): 81–98.

Shakya, Tsering. 1999. *The Dragon in the Land of Snows: A History of Modern Tibet since 1947*. New York: Penguin Compass.

Shih, Victor, Mingxing Liu, and Qi Zhang. 2007. "Placating Credible Rebels: Chinese Transfer Payments to Religious and Non-Religious Minorities." Unpublished Paper. August 14.

Sichuan Research Group. 2001. "Zhengque fenxi he chuli quntixing tufa shijian" [Investigative Report on Correctly Analyzing and Handling of Collective Protests]. In *Organization department of the Chinese Communist Party*, ed.

Zhongguo Diaocha Baogao. Xinxingshi Xia Renmin Neibu Maodun Yanjiu [China Investigative Report 2000–2001]. Beijing: Central Compilation and Translation Press.

Song, Qing, Zangzang Zhang, Bian Qiao, Qingsheng Gu, and Zhengyu Tang [宋强、张藏藏、乔边、古清生、汤正宇]. 1996. 中国可以说不 [*China Can Say No*]. 北京: 工商出版社[Beijing: Industry and Commerce Publishing House].

State Statistics Bureau. 2001. *2000 Population Census of China*. http://www.stats.gov.cn/tjsj/ndsj/renkoupucha/2000pucha/pucha.htm, checked June 27, 2008.

———. 2007. 中华人民共和国2006年国民经济和社会发展统计公报 [*2006 Economic and Social Indicators of China*]. Beijing: China Statistics Press.

Surna and Sarge [苏日娜、赛尔格]. 2005. "蒙古流动人口的婚姻家庭状况: 以内蒙古呼和浩特市为例" [The Marriage Situation of the Floating Population Among the Mongolians]. 中央民族大学学报(哲学社会科学版) [*Journal of the Central University for Nationalities (Philosophy and Social Sciences Edition)*], 32(6): 65–9.

Tang, Wenfang. 2005. *Public Opinion and Political Change in China*. Stanford, CA: Stanford University Press.

Teague, Matthew. 2009. "The Other Tibet," *National Geographic Magazine*, December.

Teng, Xing [腾星]. 2005. 《文化变迁与双语教育——凉山彝族社区教育人类学的田野工作与文本撰述》 [*Cultural Chang and Bilingual Education in Liangshan*]. 北京: 教育科学出版社 [Beijing: Education and Science Publishing House].

Togan, Isenbike. 1992. "Islam in a Changing Society: The Khojas of Eastern Turkistan." In Jo-Ann Gross, ed. Muslims in *Central Asia: Expressions of Identity and Change*. Durham, NC: Duke University Press.

Wang, Junmin [王俊敏]. 1999. "蒙、满、回、汉四族通婚研究: 呼和浩特市区的个案" [Study of Intermarriage Among the Mongolian, Manchu, Hui and Han Nationalities: Cases in Hohhot]. 西北民族研究 [*N. W. Minorities Research*] 24(1): 158–69.

———. 2003. "Ethnic Groups in Hohhot: Migration, Settlement, and Intergroup Exchanges." In Robyn Iredale, Naran Bilik, and Fei Guo, eds. *China's Minorities on the Move: Selected Case Studies*. New York: M.E. Sharpe.

Wang, Shaoguang. 2004. "For National Unity: The Political Logic of Fiscal Transfer in China." In Leong H. Liew and Shaoguang Wang, eds. *Nationalism, Democracy and National Integration in China*. New York and London: RoutledgeCurzon.

Wang, Xiaoyan [王晓燕]. 2006. "论回族婚姻及 "女子不嫁外" 婚俗" [Within Group Marriage Among the Huis]. 西北民族大学学报(哲学社会科学版) [*Journal of Northwest University for Nationalities (Philosophy and Social Science)*], 4: 57–62.

Wiemer, Calla. 2004. "The Economy of Xinjiang." In S. Frederick Starr, ed. *Xinjiang: China's Muslim Borderland*. New York: M.E. Sharpe.

Williams, C.H. 1984. "More Than Tongues Can Tell: Linguistic Factors in Ethnic Separatism." In J. Edwards, ed. *Linguistic Minorities, Policies, and Pluralism.* London: Academic Press.

Wong, Edward. 2009. "Rumbles on the Rim of China's Empire," *New York Times,* July 11.

Xie, Lei [谢蕾]. 2006. "藏汉通婚的文化整合及演变" [Tibetan and Han Intermarriage]. 内江师范学院学报 [*Journal of Neijiang Teachers College*] 21(1): 147–9.

Xinjiang Research Group. 2001. "Guanyu zhengque renshi he chuli xinxingshi xia xinjiang minzu wenti de diaocha baogao" [Investigative Report on Correctly Understanding and Handling of the Ethnic Issue in Xinjiang]. In *Organization Department of the Chinese Communist Party,* ed. Zhongguo Diaocha Baogao. Xinxingshi Xia Renmin Neibu Maodun Yanjiu [China Investigative Report 2000–2001]. Beijing: Central Compilation and Translation Press.

Xu, Ben. 2001. "Chinese Populist Nationalism: Its Intellectual Politics and Moral Dilemma." *Representations* 76(1): 120–40.

Xu, Zhenming [许振明]. 2005. "夏河县拉卜楞镇族际通婚状况调查" [Survey on Interethnic Marriage in Labrang Township, Xiahe County]. 甘肃社会科学 [*Gansu Social Sciences*], 6: 192–5.

Yang, Deliang [杨德亮]. 2005. "婚姻制度, 族群意识, 文化认同: 回族内婚姻制的历史成因和文化内涵" [Marriage System, Ethnic Awareness, Culture Identity]. 西北第二民族学院学报 [*Journal of the Second Northwest University for Nationalities*], 65(1): 53–7.

Yao, Wei, and Yueyong Ma [姚维、马岳勇]. 2005. 新疆少数民族社会心态与民族地区发展研究 [*Social Mood Among Ethnic Minorities in Xinjiang*]. 乌鲁木齐: 新疆人民出版社 [Urumqi: Xinjiang People's Publishing House].

Yardley, Jim. 2006. "A Spectator's Role for China's Muslims," *New York Times,* February 19.

Yee, Herbert S. 2005. "Ethnic Consciousness and Identity: A Research Report on Uygur-Han Relations in Xinjiang." *Asian Ethnicity* 6(1): 35–50.

Yu, Changjiang. 2006. "Life in Lara Village, Tibet." In Barry Sautman and June Teufel Dreyer, eds. *Contemporary Tibet: Politics, Development, and Society in a Disputed Region.* New York: M.E. Sharpe.

Zhang, Yuxin [张羽新]. 1988. 清政府与喇嘛教 [*Qing Government and Lamaism*]. 拉萨: 西藏人民出版社 [Lhasa: Tibet People's Publishing House].

Zhao, Yuntian [赵云田]. 1995. "《蒙古律例》和《理藩院则例》" [Mongol Law and the Regulations of the Council of Colonial Affairs]. 清史研究 [*Studies in Qing History*], 3: 106–10.

Zhou, Minglang. 2000. "Language Policy and Illiteracy in Ethnic Minority Communities in China." *Journal of Multilingual and Multicultural Development* 21(2): 129–48.

———, ed. 2004. *Language Policy in the People's Republic of China: Theory and Practice since 1949.* Boston: Kluwer Academic Publishers.

Zhu, Zhiyong. 2007. *State Schooling and Ethnic Identity.* Lanham, MD: Lexington Books.

Acknowledgments

We wish to thank the Freeman Foundation for providing Wenfang Tang with a generous research grant for the 2006–2007 Chinese Ethnicity Surveys and for visits to Xinjiang, Tibet, Yunnan, Inner Mongolia, and the Mongolian People's Republic in 2005, 2006, 2007, and 2008. We also want to thank Sun Yat-Sen University for the Project 985 Research Grant that allowed Gaochao He to participate in this project and to conduct field work in Tibet and Xinjiang. Several people made helpful comments and suggestions on the earlier drafts, including Evelyn Rawski, Victor Shih, Vicki Hesli, and Rebecca Clothey. We would also like to thank Professor Li Yan at Xinjiang Medical University and several graduate students at Sun Yat-Sen University for assisting in the surveys, including Zou Yue and Huang Yan. Pengyu Chen at the University of Iowa also provided valuable research assistance.

Policy Studies series

A publication of the East-West Center

Series Editors: Edward Aspinall and Dieter Ernst
Publications Coordinator: Carol Wong

Description

Policy Studies provides policy-relevant scholarly analysis of key contemporary domestic and international issues affecting Asia. The editors invite contributions on Asia's economics, politics, security, and international relations.

Notes to Contributors

Submissions may take the form of a proposal or complete manuscript. For more information on the Policy Studies series, please contact the Series Editors.

Editors, *Policy Studies*
East-West Center
1601 East-West Road
Honolulu, Hawai'i 96848-1601
Tel: 808.944.7197
Publications@EastWestCenter.org
EastWestCenter.org/policystudies

www.ingramcontent.com/pod-product-compliance
Lightning Source LLC
Chambersburg PA
CBHW060632280326
41933CB00012B/2015